WITH A
GRAPHIC NOVEL
IN EVERY UNIT!

GLENCOE
Backpack
Reader

COURSE 3 BOOK 1

www.glencoe.com

Mc
Graw
Hill Glencoe

New York, New York   Columbus, Ohio   Chicago, Illinois   Peoria, Illinois   Woodland Hills, California

Acknowledgments

Grateful acknowledgment is given authors, publishers, photographers, museums, and agents for permission to reprint the following copyrighted material. Every effort has been made to determine copyright owners. In case of any omissions, the Publisher will be pleased to make suitable acknowledgments in future editions.
Acknowledgments continued on page R3.

Glencoe

The *McGraw·Hill* Companies

Send all inquiries to:
Glencoe/McGraw-Hill
8787 Orion Place
Columbus, OH 43240-4027
ISBN: 978-0-07-874336-8
MHID: 0-07-874336-2
Printed in the United States of America.

3 4 5 6 7 8 9 110/055 10 09 08 07

Table of Contents

Table of Contents

 UNIT 3 **When is the price too high?**_____ **128**

Reading: What's in it for you?

*As you read the following selections, you will begin to see many possible answers to the question: **Reading: What's in it for you?** Each selection will give you a glimpse of how reading can affect you.*

As you read the selections in this unit, apply these reading skills.

- **Setting a Purpose for Reading** Before you start reading a selection, look at the title and read the brief introduction. Think about what you want to find out as you read the selection.
- **Connecting** Finding links between what you read and your own life experiences can make the selections more meaningful to you.
- **Activating Prior Knowledge** Use your own knowledge and experiences to help you understand what you are reading.
- **Identifying Author's Purpose** As you read, think about why the author wrote the selection. Authors may write to entertain, persuade, describe, or inform.

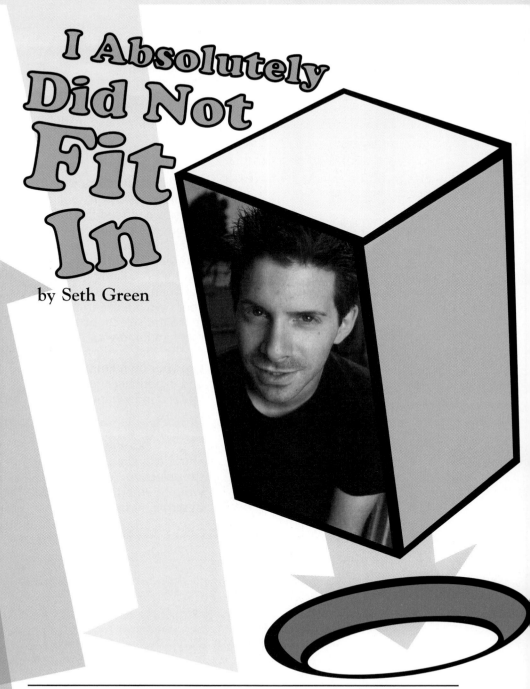

I Absolutely Did Not Fit In

by Seth Green

Find out why actor Seth Green knows exactly what it's like to be on the outside.

"I was teased about everything."

"Kids tend to make fun of what they don't have or understand, and that pretty much describes everything about me when I was a kid. I was an actor, but I didn't live in Hollywood or any other place you might be among other working kids. I lived and went to public school in Philadelphia. So I was pretty much the only kid who was out of class a lot, running to New York City to go on auditions or off to Los Angeles to film a movie. I was teased about everything. ❶

❶ Setting a Purpose for Reading
What do you want to learn about Seth Green as you read this selection?

"But that wasn't the only reason kids teased and resented me. I got it for my size, my energy, and if we're honest here, my personality: I thought I was much smarter than I was. And I let everyone know it.

"I'm five feet four inches now and, as you can guess, I've always been short. Shorter than most of the boys in my class and shorter even than some of the girls. That became glaringly apparent early on, because I was also a year accelerated, in with kids a year older than I. So not only was I the smallest, I was also the youngest.

"To the other kids, I also had a funny name. It was like, in my neighborhood at that time if you weren't Jimmy or Matt, if you didn't sound like a tough guy, you weren't in. To them, my name was weird. They'd call me Death instead of Seth. It didn't help that I didn't play athletics at school. Whenever it was my turn in kickball, everybody moved in closer.

"Even my bright red hair was cause for <u>ridicule</u>. So I was the short, unathletic kid with the red hair and funny name who was always leaving school for acting jobs. It was like I was asking for trouble—asking to be branded different.

Vo•cab•u•lary

ridicule (RID ih kyool) the act of exposing to laughter

"But that wasn't even all of it. I cop to it: I was <u>obnoxious</u>, too. My parents instilled me and my sister with a strong vocabulary, and sometimes I felt I knew more than the teachers did. You can imagine how *that* went over. I'd debate them—no teacher appreciated it. But I was self-righteous and would not be quiet. You have no idea how many times I'd hear, 'You're not being paid [to talk] now, Seth, so shut up.'

"That was at the heart of another problem. The being-a-child-actor part. If I talked about what I was doing, what movie or commercial even, I'd get <u>ostracized</u>. If I didn't talk about it, I'd get accused of being stuck-up—like I was too good to discuss it with them. It hurt. I felt like I should change somehow, but I had no idea how to make kids like me.

"Then, on the other hand, there was the part of my life when I was *in* the acting world. There, I was being praised for and having success because of the same traits I got put down for at school. For being talkative, <u>articulate</u>, a wise guy. For having red hair [which is always in demand for kids in commercials]. Even being smaller than most kids my age worked for me. As a child actor, you can play a wider range of parts for a longer period of time.

"So on the one hand, famous people like Woody Allen, for whom I starred in the movie *Radio Days*, and Johnny Carson (I was on *The Tonight Show* when I was a kid) were going on about how great I was. And on the other, everyone in school couldn't stand me."

The more you try to fit in, the more outside you are

"Mostly, I didn't dress like the other kids either. I was wearing huge, oversized army pants, T-shirts with comic book characters on them. The other kids were all very fashionable, preppy but hip. They'd wear nice pants like khakis, sweatshirts, sneakers. Some of them wore gold chains.

Vo•cab•u•lary

obnoxious (ub NAHK shus) annoying; objectionable
ostracized (AW struh syzd) excluded from a group
articulate (ar TIK yoo lut) able to express oneself easily and clearly

"I wanted to belong. I wanted to play with them, to be cool.

"So in junior high school, I went through a phase where I tried hard to fit in, by dressing and acting like them. It was the worst thing I could have done. Because kids can smell a phony a mile away. And the more you try to fit in, the more outside you're going to appear. ❷ The more cool I tried to be, the less cool I ultimately was. It took a long time for me to realize that there was nothing wrong with me. And I didn't need to feel stupid or to change in any way.

❷ **Connecting**
Do you agree with the writer's statement? Why or why not?

"There was one area where not being one of the guys served me well. That was with girls. I've always been really <u>flirtatious</u> and always had a keen respect for girls. So, like, at a school dance, when the boys stick to one side of the room and the girls huddle in the other? I would be the one guy who crosses the floor and asks someone to dance. I always knew that girls are as scared as boys, they just want the guys to make the first move. They want to have fun."

What made all the difference: making one friend

"There were two changes in my life that really turned things around for me. They both happened around the age of fourteen. The first was outside of school. I joined a youth group and started to do things I really enjoyed. We went on retreats, we'd go to Washington, D.C., to lobby for bills

Vo•cab•u•lary

flirtatious (flur TAY shus) liking to flirt with people

we wanted passed, we'd go on trips to the Pocono Mountains, we'd run dances and sleepovers and see *The Rocky Horror Picture Show*, stuff like that. For the first time in my life I was having fun with kids who liked the same things I did. And being with them helped me find myself. Maybe more importantly, for the first time in my life I was in a place where you weren't picked on for what you looked like or for what your interests were. If you were ragged on, it was because you deserved it. Because you did something evil to someone else, hurt someone else. It was never for having red hair or a 'funny' name, or being short, or being an actor.

"The second thing that happened was in school. I finally found one kid—one friend—who understood me, who felt, dressed, and acted pretty much the same way. He wasn't a working actor, but he was into comic books and music like I was.

He and I dressed the same way—when I look back, it hits me how ridiculous we must've looked. We'd wear these loud, multicolored clothes under huge black overcoats with fingerless gloves.

"We weren't trying to make a statement, and we certainly weren't trying to fit in. We were just being ourselves. And in the end, that's really what made all the difference. Because as soon as I stopped trying to fit in, everything suddenly came together—I did fit in. After a while, all the girls got into us. And at the age of fifteen, sixteen, that was more important than anything else."

"...It's okay to be geeky. It's okay to be an outsider."

"Okay, here's what I've learned. Like I said before, kids make fun of what they don't have, don't understand, or are afraid of. When you're young, similarities is all you have, so it's what you cling to. So if someone points and yells out, 'That guy's fat!' or 'That guy's a weirdo!' you'd rather belong to the group doing the criticizing than be the poor soul who's getting pointed at.

"But still, I've learned that it's better to be true to yourself—no matter how different other kids say you are—than to try and copy them. It's not the same as taking the offensive attitude of, 'Forget them, I'll do what I want, and I don't care about anyone else.' It's about doing stuff, wearing things, being among people who make you happy, without being disrespectful to others.

"My best advice? Recognize that what you've got is special, no matter how different you look or feel from other kids around you. Work really hard at what you love, and just know that it's okay to be geeky. It's okay to be an outsider. It's okay to be you. Take it from me." **3** ○

3 Identifying Author's Purpose
Why do you think Seth Green wrote this article?

Answering the BIG Question

As you do the following activities, consider the Big Question:
Reading: What's in it for you?

WRITE TO LEARN Think about a time in your life when you felt like you did not fit in. Write a brief entry in your Learner's Notebook explaining the situation. Tell how you felt about it, and what you learned from the experience.

PARTNER TALK Work with a partner who has read this selection. Discuss what the author learned about fitting in. Focus on how these lessons might help you cope if you are ever in a situation where you don't fit in.

Hunting Rattlesnakes

by Marjorie Kinnan Rawlings

What happens when your greatest fear is right in front of you and you are not ready to face it?

Ross[1] and I drove to Arcadia in his <u>coupe</u> on a warm January day.

I said, "How will you bring back the rattlesnakes?"

. . . .

[1] Ross Allen is a <u>herpetologist</u> from Florida.

Vo•cab•u•lary

herpetologist (hur puh TAWL uh jist) scientist who studies reptiles and amphibians
coupe (koop) a two-door automobile

"In the back of my car."

My courage was not adequate to inquire whether they were thrown in loose and might be expected to appear between our feet. Actually, a large portable box of heavy close-meshed wire made a safe cage. Ross wanted me to write an article about his work and on our way to the unhappy hunting grounds I took notes on a mass of data that he had accumulated in years of herpetological research. The scientific and <u>dispassionate</u> <u>detachment</u> of the material and the man made a desirable approach to rattlesnake territory. As I had discovered with the insects and <u>varmints</u>, it is difficult to be afraid of anything about which enough is known, and Ross' facts were fresh from the laboratory.

The hunting ground was Big Prairie, south of Arcadia and west of the northern tip of Lake Okeechobee. Big Prairie is a desolate cattle country, half marsh, half pasture, with islands of palm trees and cypress and oaks. At that time of year the cattlemen and Indians were burning the country, on the theory that the young fresh wire grass that springs up from the roots after a fire is the best cattle forage. Ross planned to hunt his rattlers in the forefront of the fires. They lived in winter, he said, in gopher holes, coming out in the midday warmth to <u>forage</u>, and would move ahead of the flames and be easily taken. We joined forces with a big man named Will, his snake-hunting companion of the territory, and set out in early morning, after a long rough drive over deep-rutted roads into the open wilds.

I hope never in my life to be so frightened as I was in those first few hours. ❶ I kept on Ross' footsteps, I moved

❶ **Connecting**
Have you ever been as frightened as the author was?

Vo•cab•u•lary

dispassionate (dis PASH uh nut) not affected by passion, emotion, or bias
detachment (di TATCH munt) a cool, unemotional attitude
varmints (VAR mints) animals that are considered undesirable or troublesome
forage (FOR uj) look or search for food

when he moved, sometimes jolting into him when I thought he might leave me behind. He does not use the forked stick of conventional snake hunting, but a steel prong, shaped like an L, at the end of a long stout stick. He hunted casually, calling my attention to the varying vegetation, to hawks overhead, to a pair of the rare whooping cranes that flapped over us. In mid-morning he stopped short, dropped his stick, and brought up a five-foot rattlesnake draped limply over the steel L. It seemed to me that I should drop in my tracks.

"They're not active at this season," he said quietly. "A snake takes on the temperature of its surroundings. They can't stand too much heat for that reason, and when the weather is cool, as now, they're <u>sluggish</u>."

The sun was bright overhead, the sky a <u>translucent</u> blue, and it seemed to me that it was warm enough for any snake to do as it willed. The sweat poured down my back. Ross dropped the rattler in a crocus sack and Will carried it. By noon, he had caught four. I felt faint and ill. We stopped by a pond and went swimming. The region was flat, the horizon limitless, and as I came out of the cool blue water I expected to find myself surrounded by a ring of rattlers. There were only Ross and Will, opening the lunch basket. I could not eat. Will went back and drove his truck closer, for Ross expected the hunting to be better in the afternoon. The hunting was much better. When we went back to the truck to deposit two more rattlers in the wire cage, there was a rattlesnake lying under the truck.

Ross said, "Whenever I leave my car or truck with snakes already in it, other rattlers always appear. I don't know whether this is because they scent or sense the presence of other snakes, or whether in this <u>arid</u> area they come to the car for shade in the heat of the day."

Vo•cab•u•lary

sluggish (SLUG ish) slow; showing little activity
translucent (trans LOO sunt) able to be penetrated by light
arid (AIR ud) very dry; usually describes a climate

The problem was scientific, but I had no interest. **❷**

❷ Identifying Author's Purpose
Why does the author include this statement?

That night Ross and Will and I camped out in the vast spaces of the Everglades prairies. We got water from an abandoned well and cooked supper under buttonwood bushes by a flowing stream. The camp fire blazed cheerfully under the stars and a new moon lifted in the sky. Will told tall tales of the cattlemen and the Indians and we were at peace.

Ross said, "We couldn't have a better night for catching water snakes."

After the rattlers, water snakes seemed <u>innocuous</u> enough. We worked along the edge of the stream and here Ross did not use his L-shaped steel. He reached under rocks and along the edge of the water and brought out harmless reptiles with his hands. I had said nothing to him of my fears, but he understood them. He brought a small dark snake from under a willow root.

"Wouldn't you like to hold it?" he asked. "People think snakes are cold and clammy, but they aren't. Take it in your hands. You'll see that it is warm."

Again, because I was ashamed, I took the snake in my hands. It was not cold, it was not clammy, and it lay trustingly in my hands, a thing that lived and breathed and had mortality like the rest of us. I felt an <u>upsurgence</u> of spirit.

The next day was magnificent. The air was crystal, the sky was aquamarine, and the far horizon of palms and oaks lay against the sky. I felt a new boldness and followed Ross bravely. He was making the rounds of the gopher holes. The rattlers came out in the mid-morning warmth and were never far away. He could tell by their trails whether one had come out or was still in the hole. Sometimes the two men dug the snake out. At times it was down

Vo•cab•u•lary

innocuous (in AWK yoo us) harmless
upsurgence (up SUR juns) a strong welling up

so long and winding a tunnel that the digging was hopeless. Then they blocked the entrance and went on to other holes. In an hour or so they made the original rounds, unblocking the holes. The rattler in every case came out hurriedly, as though anything were preferable to being shut in. All the time Ross talked to me, telling me the scientific facts he had discovered about the habits of the rattlers.

"They pay no attention to a man standing perfectly still," he said, and proved it by letting Will unblock a hole while he stood at the entrance as the snake came out. It was exciting to watch the snake crawl slowly beside and past the man's legs. When it was at a safe distance he walked within its range of vision, which he had proved to be no higher than a man's knee, and the snake whirled and drew back in an attitude of fighting defense. The rattler strikes only for paralyzing and killing its food, and for defense. **3**

3 Activating Prior Knowledge
How much do you know about rattlesnakes?

"It is a slow and heavy snake," Ross said. "It lies in wait on a small game trail and strikes the rat or rabbit passing by. It waits a few minutes, then follows along the trail, coming to the small animal, now dead or dying. It noses it from all sides, making sure that it is its own kill, and that it is dead and ready for swallowing."

A rattler will lie quietly without revealing itself if a man passes by and it thinks it is not seen. It slips away without fighting if given the chance. Only Ross' sharp eyes sometimes picked out the gray and yellow diamond pattern, camouflaged among the grasses. In the cool of the morning, chilled by the January air, the snakes showed no fight. They could be looped up limply over the steel L and dropped in a sack or up into the wire cage on the back of Will's truck. As the sun mounted in the sky and warmed the moist Everglades earth, the snakes were warmed too, and Ross warned that it was time to go more cautiously. Yet having learned that it was we who were the aggressors; that immobility meant complete safety; that the snakes, for all their lightning flash in striking, were inaccurate in their aim, with limited vision;

having watched again and again the liquid grace of movement, the beauty of pattern, suddenly I understood that I was drinking in freely the magnificent sweep of the horizon, with no fear of what might be at the moment under my feet. I went off hunting by myself, and though I found no snakes, I should have known what to do.

The sun was dropping low in the west. Masses of white cloud hung above the flat marshy plain and seemed to be tangled in the tops of distant palms and cypresses. The sky turned orange, then saffron. I walked leisurely back toward the truck. In the distance I could see Ross and Will making their way in too. The season was more advanced than at [Cross] Creek, two hundred miles to

---

Vo•cab•u•lary

saffron (SAF run) deep orange-yellow

the north, and I noticed that spring flowers were blooming among the lumpy <u>hummocks</u>. I leaned over to pick a white violet. There was a rattlesnake under the violet.

If this had happened the week before, if it had happened the day before, I think I should have lain down and died on top of the rattlesnake, with no need of being struck and poisoned. The snake did not coil, but lifted its head and whirred its rattles lightly. I stepped back slowly and put the violet in a buttonhole. I reached forward and laid the steel L across the snake's neck, just back of the blunt head. I called to Ross:

"I've got one."

He strolled toward me.

"Well, pick it up," he said.

I released it and slipped the L under the middle of the thick body.

"Go put it in the box."

He went ahead of me and lifted the top of the wire cage. I made the truck with the rattler, but when I reached up the six feet to drop it in the cage, it slipped off the stick and dropped on Ross' feet. It made no effort to strike.

"Pick it up again," he said. "If you'll pin it down lightly and reach just back of its head with your hand, as you've seen me do, you can drop it in more easily."

I pinned it and leaned over.

Vo·cab·u·lary

hummocks (HUM uks) low mounds or ridges of earth

"I'm awfully sorry," I said, "but you're pushing me a little too fast."

He grinned. I lifted it on the stick and again as I had it at head height, it slipped off, down Ross' boots and on top of his feet. He stood as still as a stump. I dropped the snake on his feet for the third time. It seemed to me that the most patient of rattlers might in time resent being hauled up and down, and for all the man's quiet certainty that in standing motionless there was no danger, would strike at whatever was nearest, and that would be Ross.

I said, "I'm just not man enough to keep this up any longer," and he laughed and reached down with his smooth quickness and lifted the snake back of the head and dropped it in the cage. It slid in among its mates and settled in a corner. The hunt was over and we drove back over the uneven trail to Will's village and left him and went on to Arcadia and home. Our catch for the two days was thirty-two rattlers.

I said to Ross, "I believe that tomorrow I could have picked up that snake."

Back at the Creek, I felt a new lightness. I had done battle with a great fear, and the victory was mine. **4** ○

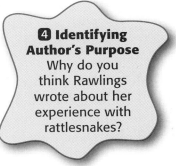

4 Identifying Author's Purpose
Why do you think Rawlings wrote about her experience with rattlesnakes?

Answering the
BIG Question

As you do the following activities, consider the Big Question:
Reading: What's in it for you?

WRITE TO LEARN Is there something that truly frightens you? Have you faced that fear or thought about doing so? Write a brief entry in your Learner's Notebook about your fear and what you have done or could do to cope with it.

LITERATURE GROUPS Join with two or three students who have read this selection. Talk about how the author faced her fears. What lessons did she learn about snakes and, more importantly, about herself? What can each of you learn by facing a fear?

42nd Street Library

by Nikki Grimes

To this speaker, the library is like a house of worship.

The library
is no place to kneel
but this cathedral of books
feels holy.
I observe
a moment of silence
at the entryway.
The librarians
like ushers
point me in
the right direction.
I've only been here
once before.
That first time
I was a human top
spinning dizzy
in the middle of the hall.
I thought all visitors
should bow
or fold their hands—

do something special.
But I was too
dazed myself
to do more than
gaze up, and up, and up
and sigh. **1**
The "Quiet" signs
posted everywhere
warned me not to speak.
And why would I want to?
It looked to me like
all the good words
were already taken.

1 Connecting
Have you ever visited a place that caused you to have feelings like those of the speaker?

COMPANION

by Manjush Dasgupta
India
Translated by the poet

Who will be your companion when no one else is around?

I said, I won't read
Butterflies do not read
Rivers do not
Nor does the ocean
Even the stars do not read.

Mummy said, I read
Your grandpa reads
So does your father
And millions of other people
Why would you remain different?

I said, I would play
Play with the butterfly
And float paper boats in the stream
Stars would decorate them.

Now Mummy is no more
Father is away
I am sick
I read and only read
Books are brooks to me.

THE LIST

by Naomi Shihab Nye

Is it possible to think too much about books?

A man told me he had calculated
the exact number of books
he would be able to read before he died
by figuring the average number
of books he read per month
and his probable earth span,
(averaging how long
his dad and grandpa had lived,
adding on a few years since he
exercised more than they did).
Then he made a list of necessary books,
nonfiction mostly, history, philosophy,
fiction and poetry from different time periods
so there wouldn't be large gaps in his mind.

He had given up <u>frivolous</u> reading entirely.
There are only so many days.

Oh I felt sad to hear such an organized plan.
What about the books that aren't written yet,
the books his friends might recommend
that aren't on the list,
the yummy magazine that might fall
into his view at a silly moment after all?
What about the mystery search
through <u>delectable</u> library shelves?
I felt the heartbeat of forgotten precious books
calling for his hand. ❷ ○

> **❷ Identifying Author's Purpose**
> What main idea does the poet want to communicate in this poem?

Answering the BIG Question

As you do the following activities, consider the Big Question:
Reading: What's in it for you?

WRITE TO LEARN The three poems all express ideas about books and reading. Which ideas do you relate to the most, and why? Write your response in your Learner's Notebook.

PARTNER TALK Meet with a classmate who has read these poems. Role-play a conversation between the man and the speaker in "The List." Try to convince the other person that your attitude toward reading is the right one.

Vo•cab•u•lary

frivolous (FRIV uh lus) inappropriately silly
delectable (duh LEK tuh bul) delicious, tasty; wonderful

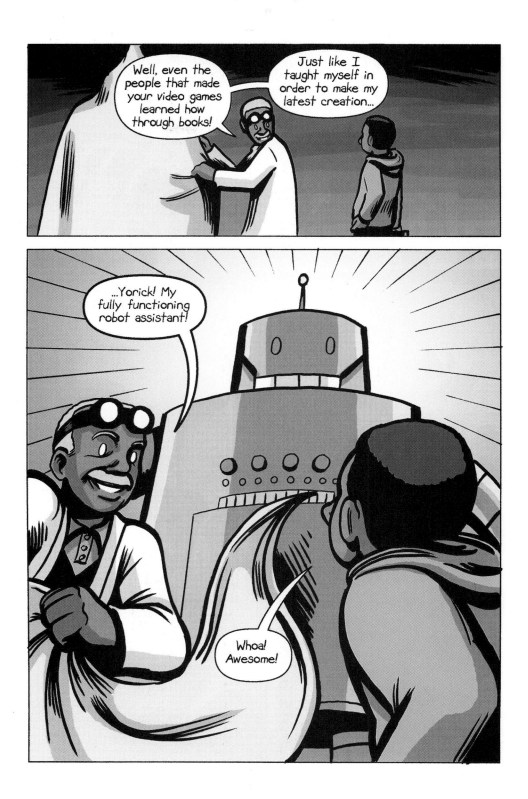

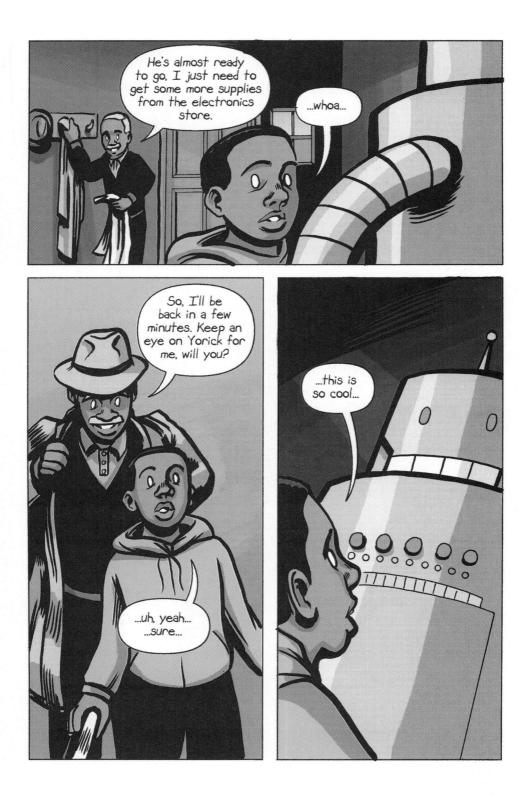

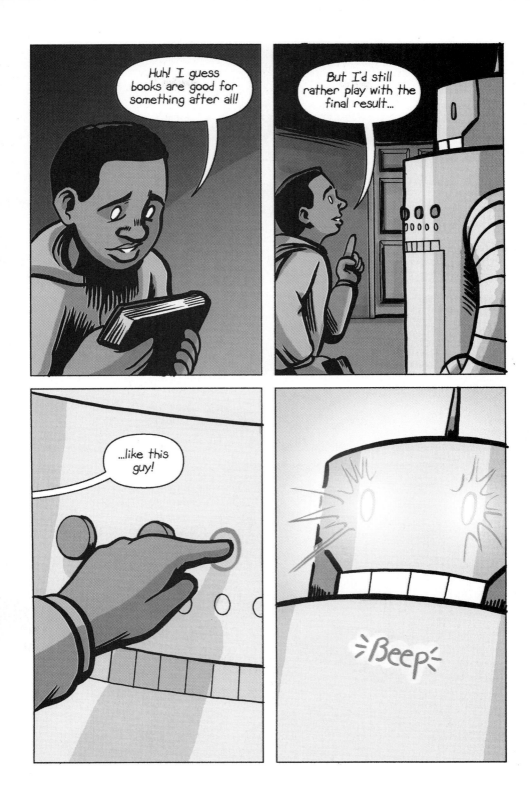

WRITE TO LEARN
Yorick's user manual helps Sam figure out what he needs to stop Yorick. Think about the many kinds of books, manuals, labels, and other things you need to read just to get through a week. Make a list in your Learner's Notebook.

Bodies of Pompeii

by Jason Urbanus

What happened to the people of Pompeii when the deadly volcano erupted?

When Mount Vesuvius erupted, not everyone was able to flee the city of Pompeii. Exactly how many people died within the city's limits is still not known. However, the dead bodies <u>excavated</u> in the past 250 years have provided valuable information about the city's final moments. **1**

Among the best-known finds at Pompeii are the eerie plaster casts of the ancient Pompeians. In the 1860s, the Italian archaeologist Giuseppe Fiorelli devised an <u>innovative</u> method using

> **1 Setting a Purpose for Reading**
> What information about Pompeii's last moments would interest you most?

Vo·cab·u·lary

excavated (EX kuh vayt ud) dug up from underground
innovative (IN uh vay tiv) new and unusual

liquid plaster to figure out what the empty spaces he had found in the ash represented.

Plaster Bodies

When Mount Vesuvius erupted almost 1,800 years earlier, it buried Pompeii under as much as 40 feet of ash. The people who had not fled the city were buried by these volcanic layers and then forgotten. In the centuries that followed, the layers of volcanic ash were pressed together into one compact layer. Over time, the flesh and skin of those who had been buried decayed so that nothing was left within the layers of ash except bones and empty air pockets.

When Fiorelli found these empty air pockets, he poured buckets of liquid plaster into each space. As the plaster dried, it took the shape of the empty air pocket. After the soil and debris around the plaster were removed, what remained was an almost perfect cast of the dead body.

From these casts, archaeologists can learn about the individual Pompeians. Personal items found alongside the bodies provide clues to the people's social status. For example, a skeleton found wearing expensive earrings and gold bracelets most likely was

a member of a rich family. On the other hand, slaves are easily identified as their bodies often had chains on either their arms or their wrists. Because the Pompeians tried to flee with their most important possessions, the objects found lying in areas where the dead were found sometimes reveal a person's name or occupation. Indeed, some bodies were found holding their house keys.

It's Raining Ash

The bodies that have been found also tell us about Pompeii's final hours and how the people died. Some died indoors when buildings in which they had taken shelter collapsed as the falling ash <u>accumulated</u> on the roofs early in the eruption. Later, clouds of hot gases mixed with ash swept down the side of Vesuvius and through the town, killing any survivors. The fact that many of the bodies are covering their mouths shows that these people were unable to breathe and <u>suffocated</u> before being covered with ash. ○

Answering the BIG Question

As you do the following activities, consider the Big Question:
Reading: What's in it for you?

WRITE TO LEARN When people are in danger, they often try to save things that are important to them. Some of the people in Pompeii grabbed their house keys. What would you reach for? Write a brief entry in your Learner's Notebook about several items you would want to save and why they are important to you.

PARTNER TALK Talk with another student who has read this selection. Discuss what it must have been like for the people of Pompeii when Mount Vesuvius erupted. Compare your lists of items you would want to save. Explain why you chose those specific things.

Vo·cab·u·lary

accumulated (uh KYOO myoo layt ud) collected or gathered together
suffocated (SUF uh kayt ud) killed or died from lack of oxygen and ability to breathe

FROM **Maizon at Blue Hill**

by Jacqueline Woodson

Find out what it means to one girl to be the only African-American at her school.

"**Y**ou have brothers and sisters, Maizon?" Sandy asked.

"Nope," I said, annoyed that she had broken through my thoughts. "Just me."

"Sometimes I wish I was an only child. I have two older sisters and two younger brothers," she confided.

"Middle child."

"I guess."

"Are they all in boarding school?" **1**

In the darkness, I could see the shadow of Sandy raising up on her elbow. "Nope, just me. Blue Hill gave me a track scholarship disguised as an academic one."

"I didn't know you were on scholarship. I thought I was the only one."

"Are you kidding? Last year Blue Hill gave out fifty-four academic scholarships. Diana Cortez has one. She's a junior. So do my friends Sonia Chan and Gayle Childs—and Sara

> **1 Activating Prior Knowledge**
> Think about what you know about life at boarding school.

Carmona is on scholarship. But they're on different ones than me. Mine isn't for grades. I did lousy in grade school. But I made All-State in the quarter mile and I led my softball team to the championships. The paper wrote articles about me. You play sports?"

"Not really."

"You look like you'd be good in basketball. You're so tall and thin."

I felt a flicker of warmth toward Sandy. I had only been called "skinny," never "thin."

"I'm not coordinated. I mean, sometimes I am, but not a lot. Plus, I don't think I'd be good at team sports. I'm sort of an individual."

"That's 'cause you're an only child. My *family* is a team sport. I mean, there're so many of us." Sandy lay back down.

My mind was spinning a little bit. I hadn't even thought that Sandy was on scholarship. I knew I hadn't thought about it because she was white and I just figured that no white people would need help paying for Blue Hill. A long time ago, Ms. Dell had sat me and Margaret down in her kitchen with bowls of her famous Jell-O with cherries in front of us.

"You're gonna learn about racism and death and pain before you're teenagers," she warned. Margaret and I had nodded. By then we knew Ms. Dell had the gift to see into the future. "I'm gonna tell you this," Ms. Dell continued. "Racism doesn't know color, death doesn't know age, and pain doesn't know might."

Lying there, I wondered if it was racist of me to think all white people were rich.

Sandy's breathing slowed. After a while, when I couldn't hear it at all, I knew she was asleep.

I lay awake for a long time. What was it that made white people strange to me, that made Charli and Sheila and Marie seem threatening and safe at the same time? Why hadn't I asked myself these questions before?

"Because you never had to," I heard Ms. Dell murmur

somewhere between my waking and sleeping.

Mr. Parsons hadn't lied about small classes. There were only twelve girls in my math class, eight in science, eight in French, nine in geography, and fourteen girls in my last class of the day, English. English class met in Laremy Hall, the gabled building I could see from my dorm window. It was right next to the main hall. We sat in a semicircle on the hardwood floor. Our teacher, Mrs. Dexter, wore a poncho and her hair cut short. She sat cross-legged at the opening of the circle. After we had gone around and introduced ourselves, Mrs. Dexter started talking. We would be doing Shakespeare this year, she promised. The class groaned. I hated the little bit of Shakespeare I had read.

"What's all the groaning?" Mrs. Dexter asked, smiling.

The class was silent.

"Can't he get his point across in fewer words?" I asked.

The class laughed. Some girls nodded.

For the next half hour we discussed what we'd be reading—*The Lottery, Animal Farm, A Light in the Forest, A Separate Peace,* and a bunch of other books I hadn't heard of. But other girls in the class seemed to know everything about every book already. I listened to them, embarrassed that I had nothing to contribute, promising myself I'd start in on those books the minute I had a chance.

Then Mrs. Dexter asked us to choose a book we'd like to read in class. Everyone named their favorite book. Mrs. Dexter said some books people suggested were too easy. They got the ax.

"What about you, Maizon?"

I thought for a moment, feeling everyone's eyes on me. "I read a book last summer called *The Bluest Eye,* by a woman named Toni Morrison. I'd want to read that again." **2**

Mrs. Dexter nodded. "That's a marvelous book," she said, and I felt myself grow warm. She wrote our suggestions down on a stray piece of looseleaf paper.

2 Connecting
What book would you choose?

"We're going to start with your suggestions," she said to the class. "Then we'll do my reading."

The class groaned again, but underneath the complaining I could feel everybody's excitement, especially my own. I couldn't wait to reread *The Bluest Eye*.

After English, I made my way back to the main hall for the debate meeting. Some of the cross-country team were already doing half-mile sprints on the field. I watched them for a moment, wondering why anyone got a thrill running back and forth. Running only made me tired. Charli rushed by in her field hockey skirt.

"Miss Norman said to tell you to come by tomorrow if you have any interest in playing junior varsity."

I nodded.

"I help her coach them sometimes," Charli called, taking off into a jog. She lifted her shades and winked. "They're so cute and tiny," she mocked. I rolled my eyes. I hated being the youngest person, anywhere.

"Hey, Maizon!" Sybil said, opening the door and stepping back to allow me to enter. The room was a corner one, surrounded by windows and covered with dark blue carpeting. The windows let in a lot of sun. There were pictures of explorers on the wall. Chairs were set up in a semicircle the way they had been in all of my classes, except English, where there were no chairs. As I stood in front of one to peel my knapsack from my shoulders, the rest of the girls in the circle stared at me.

"Hi," I said softly, feeling strange. "Hi everybody."

"Hey, Maizon," different people murmured. I recognized a few of the faces from different classes, but only knew two or three names.

"We've been talking about some of the issues we're going to be debating this year," Sybil said brightly. "But now, I guess, since this is everyone, I hope, we should give our names and stuff before we go on."

I nodded, figuring she was leading the group.

"I'm Maizon," I said, nodding toward the circle. "I'm a lower school freshman."

The group murmured a hello and similar introductions followed.

"You're the only freshman, Maizon," Sybil said, after all the introductions had been made.

"I'm used to being the only someone," I said.

The other girls laughed uneasily. I shrugged. The room suddenly felt hot to me and I pulled my collar away from my neck a little and pushed the sleeves of my blouse up to my elbows. Everyone watched this.

"How does it feel?" someone asked me, a girl whose name I didn't remember.

I shrugged again. "I haven't really thought about it much."

"I'd be interested in knowing what it's like here, actually . . . ," Sybil said. "I mean, for you."

I said, "I'd be interested in knowing what it's like for *you*."

Sybil gave a quick look around the room and pulled her shoulders to her ears. "I don't think that would be too interesting," she said.

"Why not?"

"'Cause for me, it's the same as it is for everybody, I guess. Except you and Charli and them," she said.

"How do you know how it is for me?" The room was still. Heads had stopped moving from me to Sybil then back again and had dropped. The others listened without making their listening seem obvious. They were the heart of our conversation, the edges and the middle of it. "I mean, you and I have never even talked to each other, Sybil. That's why I want to know what it's like for you, and then I can see if it's the same for me."

Sybil looked up at me, her small dark eyes moving from one place on my face to another without meeting mine. "You know why it's different for you, Maizon," she said.

"I don't," I said, crossing my legs and leaning toward her. "I *am* smart, but I don't know everything. What makes Blue Hill so different for me?" ❸

Someone coughed. I looked over at her and she covered her mouth with her hand.

❸ **Activating Prior Knowledge**
What does the girls' body language say about what they are thinking and feeling?

I stared hard into Sybil's eyes, all the while knowing that what I was doing was wrong of me. What I saw there was Sybil's own fear of me and this made me madder than I had ever been. She had no right to have such a fear. She had never met me before, had never spoken to me or sat down beside me at dinner. It was the same fear that was in all of their eyes, but Sybil was the bravest. She was in charge and had chosen to raise her eyes and show me the fear there. I hated them all. But because she was brave, I hated Sybil the most.

"What's different?" I asked, giving a quick look around to include the others in this question. "I can't see me now, so you have to tell me, Sybil. What's so *different* about me?"

"You're black, Maizon," Sybil said. There was a near silent longing in the back of her voice. I heard her desire, if only for a moment, an hour or a day, to be who I am. In Sybil's voice I heard the part of her—of each of them sitting in the room— who had always wanted to be the special one. The one like no other, who stands out and above only because she is allowed to, only because others have chosen to shrink in her presence.

I brushed at my skirt with my hand like I was flicking lint away, but it was really the moment I was ridding myself of. I thought of Marie and how she had brushed her thigh in the same way the first day we met. I was brushing away all of them with a flick of my hand. I felt the room shrink back away from me, felt their individual disappointment and felt the new strength of this power I had discovered within myself. "Yes, I am," I said, bringing the back of my hand to my eyes as though I were checking for the first time. "I am black, aren't I?" ❹

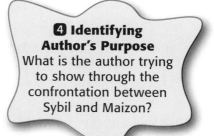

❹ Identifying Author's Purpose
What is the author trying to show through the confrontation between Sybil and Maizon?

No one said a word. I listened as someone called the meeting to order. It moved on slowly. I felt the other girls stealing glances at me. I felt mean all of a sudden. As they discussed the coming debates, my skirt had all of my attention. I stared at the dark green pleats riding along the front, at my skinny brown legs beneath it. I raised my feet in front of me and stared at my penny loafers, folded my arms across my chest, exhaled loudly to show my boredom, and gazed at the starched, white creases in the sleeves of my blouse.

It seemed like hours before Sybil adjourned the meeting. Only then, with the exits of the others, did the air in the room seem to lift.

"I hope we'll be friends, Maizon," Sybil said, when only she and I were left.

"Yeah. I hope so too." But the lie rode freely on the words, and Sybil knew it. ○

Answering the
BIG Question

As you do the following activities, consider the Big Question:
Reading: What's in it for you?

WRITE TO LEARN Have you ever been the "only someone" in a group? Write a brief entry in your Learner's Notebook about what the experience was like for you. Did you learn any lessons from the experience?

PARTNER TALK Meet with a partner who has read this selection. Talk about what role, if any, racism plays in your life. Discuss what you have learned from Maizon's experience at the debate meeting.

JUMPING OVER BOUNDARIES

by Linda Alvarado

Find out how doing the high jump started one woman on the path to success and ownership of a major-league baseball team.

When I was in elementary school, we had an annual sports day. Girls did things like hopscotch, jump rope, tetherball, and dodge ball. The boys got to do high jumping.

That's what I wanted to do—high jumping. I went to sign up.

"Girls don't do high jumping," the coach said. "Girls have all these other things they can do." ❶ He excitedly described how much fun it would be.

I'd been high jumping in the backyard with my five brothers for years. I went home and told my mother what the coach had said. My mother, a small, thin Hispanic woman only four feet eleven inches tall, said, "I think we should go visit him."

"Visit who?" I asked.

"The principal."

❶ **Connecting**
Think of a time when you were told you couldn't do something.

43

Jumping Over Boundaries

"Visit the principal?" I was terrified. Would I get in trouble? Would my mother and I be crossing boundaries we shouldn't cross?

My mom and I went to Mr. White's office. "Linda wants to do the high jump," my mother said.

"Mrs. Martinez, you don't understand. This is the tradition of our Annual Sports Day," he said.

"But Señor White, I don't know where it says that girls cannot do this."

The principal couldn't find any rules that said girls couldn't do the high jump. "I have to think about this," he said at last.

When we got home, my mom told me something I would always remember: this wasn't just about me.

"Maybe other girls want to do this, too," she said.

My mother waited a week, and then she walked over to the school. "Señor White, please. I ask you this not for me and not for Linda, but let's just see how it works."

In the end, Mr. White agreed.

As it turned out, I won the high-jumping contest. To my surprise, some of the cheers I got were from boys! My mother was right—it wasn't about me. It was about making people think about what girls could do.

High jumping helped me to understand that people would not always accept or welcome me. I used this lesson in my career as a building contractor. Just as girls did not do the high jump, women were not supposed to construct buildings.

When I first started in business, my mother would say to me in Spanish, *"Mi'jita, empieza pequeño, pero piensa grande"* (My dear little one, start small, but think big). I found small ways to begin to show what I could do. I began by installing concrete curbs, gutters, and sidewalks.

Today, my company, Alvarado Construction, builds large projects, including schools, aquariums, airports, and convention centers. I love my job. I view my career much like Robert Frost's poem. I took the path least traveled by girls and women, and this has really made a difference. ❷

> **❷ Identifying Author's Purpose**
> What is the most important thing Linda Alvarado wants you to know about her?

- While other kids baked cookies shaped like teddy bears or candy canes, Linda constructed Eiffel Tower cookies!

- As a kid, Linda loved building wood forts in the backyard. Now she builds stadiums and high-rise buildings.

- Alvarado invites inner-city kids to join her in the best seats in the stadium to watch the Colorado Rockies play baseball. How can she do that? She's one of the owners of this major league team.

- In 2003, Alvarado was inducted into the National Women's Hall of Fame. ○

Answering the BIG Question

As you do the following activities, consider the Big Question: **Reading: What's in it for you?**

WRITE TO LEARN Have you ever been told you cannot do something because of who you are? Write a brief entry in your Learner's Notebook explaining the situation and how you reacted to it. What did you learn from the experience?

LITERATURE GROUPS Meet with two or three classmates who have read this selection. Talk about how you and others have overcome obstacles that certain people tried to put in your way. How did it feel to overcome these obstacles?

MILO CONDUCTS THE DAWN

by Norton Juster
from *The Phantom Tollbooth*

Conducting the colors of the morning sky sounds exciting, but what happens when the orchestra is suddenly out of control?

Milo is a boy who doesn't know what to do with himself. Everything bores him, until one day a huge parcel arrives containing a toy tollbooth (the kind of thing you put money in when you are driving on a road or a bridge which is not publicly owned). Milo, in a bored way, pretends to put money in and pretends to drive past it. Instantly he finds himself

in the midst of strange adventures. He meets Tock, his Watchdog,
who has a large clock in one side of him, and the Humbug.
They eventually meet a boy called Alec,
whose feet never touch the ground. Alec acts
as their guide. **1**

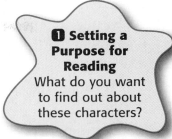

1 Setting a Purpose for Reading
What do you want to find out about these characters?

The sun was dropping slowly from sight, and stripes of purple and orange and crimson and gold piled themselves on top of the distant hills. The last shafts of light waited patiently for a flight of wrens to find their way home, and a group of anxious stars had already taken their places.

"Here we are!" cried Alec, and, with a sweep of his arm, he pointed toward an enormous symphony orchestra. "Isn't it a grand sight?"

There were at least a thousand musicians arranged in a great arc before them. To the left and right were the violins and cellos, whose bows moved in great waves, and behind them in numberless <u>profusion</u> the piccolos, flutes, clarinets, oboes, <u>bassoons</u>, horns, trumpets, trombones, and tubas were all playing at once. At the very rear, so far away that they could hardly be seen, were the percussion instruments, and lastly, in a long line up one side of a steep slope, were the solemn bass fiddles.

On a high podium in front stood the conductor, a tall, <u>gaunt</u> man with dark deep-set eyes and a thin mouth placed carelessly between his long pointed nose and his long pointed chin. He used no baton, but conducted with large, sweeping movements which seemed to start at his toes and work slowly up through his body and along his slender arms and end finally at the tips of his graceful fingers.

Vo•cab•u•lary

profusion (pruh FYOO zhun) great quantities; extravagance
bassoons (buh SOONZ) low-pitched woodwind instruments
gaunt (gawnt) thin and bony

"I don't hear any music," said Milo.

"That's right," said Alec; "you don't listen to this concert— you watch it. Now, pay attention."

As the conductor waved his arms, he molded the air like handfuls of soft clay, and the musicians carefully followed his every direction.

"What are they playing?" asked Tock, looking up <u>inquisitively</u> at Alec.

"The sunset, of course. They play it every evening, about this time."

"They do?" said Milo quizzically.

"Naturally," answered Alec; "and they also play morning, noon, and night, when of course, it's morning, noon, or night. Why, there wouldn't be any color in the world unless they played it. Each instrument plays a different one," he explained, "and depending, of course, on what season it is and how the weather's to be, the conductor chooses his score and directs the day. ❷ But watch: the sun has almost set, and in a moment you can ask Chroma himself."

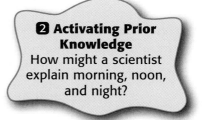

❷ Activating Prior Knowledge
How might a scientist explain morning, noon, and night?

The last colors slowly faded from the western sky, and, as they did, one by one the instruments stopped, until only the bass fiddles, in their somber slow movement, were left to play the night and a single set of silver bells brightened the constellations. The conductor let his arms fall limply at his sides and stood quite still as darkness claimed the forest.

"That was a very beautiful sunset," said Milo, walking to the <u>podium</u>.

Vo•cab•u•lary

inquisitively (in KWIZ ih tiv lee) in a curious, eager way
podium (POH dee um) raised platform for an orchestra conductor or speaker

"It should be," was the reply: "we've been practicing since the world began." And, reaching down, the speaker picked Milo off the ground and set him on the music stand. "I am Chroma the Great," he continued, gesturing broadly with his hands, "conductor of color, <u>maestro</u> of pigment, and director of the entire spectrum."

"Do you play all day long?" asked Milo when he had introduced himself.

"Ah yes, all day, every day," he sang out, then pirouetted gracefully around the platform. "I rest only at night, and even then *they* play on."

"But what would happen if you stopped?" asked Milo, who didn't quite believe that color happened like that.

"See for yourself," roared Chroma, and he raised both hands high over his head. Immediately the instruments that were playing stopped, and at once all color vanished. The world looked like an enormous coloring book that had never been used. Everything appeared in simple black outlines, and it looked as if someone with a set of paints the size of a house and a brush as wide could stay happily occupied for years. Then Chroma lowered his arms. The instruments began again and the color returned.

"You see what a dull place the world would be without color?" he said, bowing until his chin almost touched the ground. "But what pleasure to lead my violins in a <u>serenade</u> of spring green or hear my trumpets blare out the blue sea and then watch the oboes tint it all in warm yellow sunshine. And rainbows are best of all—and blazing neon signs, and taxicabs with stripes, and the soft, muted tones of a foggy day. We play them all."

While Chroma was speaking, Milo sat with his eyes open wide, and Alec, Tock, and the Humbug looked on in wonder.

Vo•cab•u•lary

maestro (MY stroh) master in an art, especially a composer, conductor, or music teacher
serenade (sair uh NAYD) a performance given to honor or express love for someone

Milo Conducts the Dawn

"Now I really must get some sleep," Chroma yawned. "We've had lightning, fireworks, and parades for the last few nights, and I've had to be up to conduct them. But tonight is sure to be quiet." Then, putting his large hand on Milo's shoulder, he said, "Be a good fellow and watch my orchestra till morning, will you? And be sure to wake me at 5:23 for sunrise. Good night, good night, good night."

With that he leaped lightly from the podium and, in three long steps, vanished into the forest.

One by one, the hours passed, and at exactly 5:22 (by Tock's very accurate clock) Milo carefully opened one eye and, in a moment, the other. Everything was still purple, dark blue, and black, yet scarcely a minute remained to the long, quiet night.

He stretched lazily, rubbed his eyelids, scratched his head, and shivered once as a greeting to the early-morning mist.

"I must wake Chroma for the sunrise," he said softly. Then he suddenly wondered what it would be like to lead the orchestra and to color the whole world himself.

The idea whirled through his thoughts until he quickly decided that since it couldn't be very difficult, and since they probably all knew what to do by themselves anyway, and since it did seem a shame to wake anyone so early, and since it might be his only chance to try, and since the musicians were already poised and ready, he would—but just for a little while. **3**

And so, as everyone slept peacefully on, Milo stood on tiptoes, raised his arms slowly in front of him, and made the slightest movement possible with the index finger of his right hand. It was now 5:23 a.m.

3 Connecting
Have you ever used reasons like Milo's to justify a decision?

As if understanding his signal perfectly, a single piccolo played a single note and off in the east a solitary shaft of cool lemon light flicked across the sky. Milo smiled happily and then cautiously crooked his finger again. This time two more piccolos and a flute joined in and three more rays of light danced lightly into view. Then with both hands he made a great circular sweep in the air and watched with delight as all the musicians began to play at once.

The cellos made the hills glow red, and the leaves and grass were tipped with a soft pale green as the violins began their song. Only the bass fiddles rested as the entire orchestra washed the forest in color.

Milo was overjoyed because they were all playing for him, and just the way they should.

"Won't Chroma be surprised?" he thought, signaling the musicians to stop. "I'll wake him now."

But, instead of stopping, they continued to play even louder than before, until each color became more brilliant than he thought possible. Milo shielded his eyes with one hand and waved the other desperately, but the colors continued to grow brighter and brighter and brighter, until an even more curious thing began to happen.

As Milo frantically conducted, the sky changed slowly from blue to tan and then to a rich magenta red. Flurries of light-green snow began to fall, and the leaves on the trees and bushes turned a vivid orange.

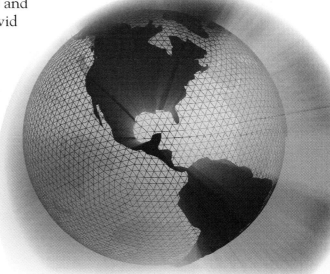

All the flowers suddenly appeared black, the gray rocks became a lovely soft <u>chartreuse</u>, and even peacefully sleeping Tock changed from brown to a

Vo·cab·u·lary

chartreuse (shar TROOZ) a bright yellow-green color

magnificent ultramarine. Nothing was the color it should have been, and yet, the more he tried to straighten things out, the worse they became.

"I wish I hadn't started," he thought unhappily as a pale-blue blackbird flew by. "There doesn't seem to be any way to stop them."

He tried very hard to do everything just the way Chroma had done, but nothing worked. The musicians played on, faster and faster, and the purple sun raced quickly across the sky. In less than a minute it had set once more in the west and then, without any pause, risen again in the east. The sky was now quite yellow and the grass a charming shade of lavender. Seven times the sun rose and almost as quickly disappeared as the colors kept changing. In just a few minutes a whole week had gone by.

At last the exhausted Milo, afraid to call for help and on the verge of tears, dropped his hands to his sides. The orchestra stopped. The colors disappeared, and once again it was night. The time was 5:27 a.m.

"Wake up, everybody! Time for the sunrise!" he shouted with relief, and quickly jumped from the music stand.

"What a marvelous rest," said Chroma, striding to the podium. "I feel as though I'd slept for a week. My, my, I see we're a little late this morning. I'll have to cut my lunch hour short by four minutes."

He tapped for attention, and this time the dawn proceeded perfectly.

"You did a fine job," he said, patting Milo on the head. "Someday I'll let you conduct the orchestra yourself."

Tock wagged his tail proudly, but Milo didn't say a word, and to this day no one knows of the lost week but the few people who happened to be awake at 5:23 on that very strange morning.

"We'd better be getting along," said Tock, whose alarm had begun to ring again, "for there's still a long way to go."

Chroma nodded a fond good-bye as they all started back through the forest, and in honor of the visit he made all the wildflowers bloom in a breathtaking display.

"I'm sorry you can't stay longer," said Alec sadly. "There's so much more to see in the Forest of Sight. But I suppose there's a lot to see everywhere, if only you keep your eyes open." **4** ○

4 Identifying Author's Purpose
Do you think the author intended to explain or to entertain?

Answering the BIG Question

As you do the following activities, consider the Big Question:
Reading: What's in it for you?

WRITE TO LEARN Have you ever tried to do something that looked easy but turned out to be complicated? Write a brief entry in your Learner's Notebook about what happened.

PARTNER TALK Meet with another student who has read this selection. Talk about how Milo handled the responsibility Chroma gave him. What might you have done differently?

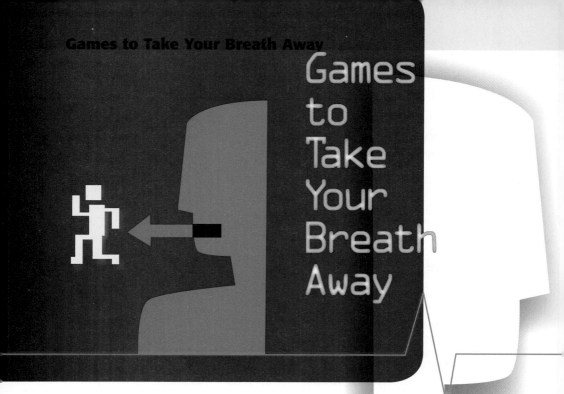

Games to Take Your Breath Away

Find out about a game you can play just by changing how you breathe.

A lot of computer games are breathtaking to play, but few more so than the one developed by scientists at Dublin's Media Lab Europe. **1**

Instead of using a joystick or mouse to control on-screen characters, the game uses <u>sensors</u> stuck to a player's body.

1 Activating Prior Knowledge
As you read, think about video games you like to play and how they make you feel.

Vo•cab•u•lary

sensors (SEN surz) devices that receive and respond to a signal

The sensors monitor breathing and only move characters on-screen if the player breathes in the right way.

The game is designed for children in hospitals to help them cope with boredom during long periods of bed rest and recuperation.

High Flyer

"The interface to the game isn't a joystick, it's your breath," said Gary McDarby, director of the Mind Games group at the Media Lab Europe.

The research group is working on ways to affect the mood of people using computers or playing games.

Techniques used by the group include immersive artificial environments, such as virtual reality, and biofeedback.

This latter approach is driving work on the Breathing Space game that tries to make players relax by forcing them to do things that calm them down.

Dr. McDarby said the game uses sensors placed on a player's waist and ribcage to measure the expansion and contraction of their diaphragm.

"The sensors on your body connect you to the video game," Dr. McDarby told the BBC programme "Go Digital."

The first versions of the game involve controlling a flying dragon on-screen and trying to make it fly along a valley passing through successive hoops of fire.

"You control the creature in the game by breathing deeply or

Vo•cab•u•lary

recuperation (ruh koo pur AY shun) the time during which a person returns to health or recovers from an injury or sickness
interface (IN tur fays) means of communication between a person and a machine
immersive (ih MUR siv) completely surrounding
biofeedback (by oh FEED bak) the technique of using monitoring devices to help people control body functions, such as breathing or blood pressure

not breathing deeply," he said.

"When you don't breathe the creature will fall down to the bottom of the valley," he said, "when you do breathe deeply it will rise up."

Deep breathing was chosen as a control technique because it is known to help people relax. Dr. McDarby said the game was designed for children in the hospital who have to stay in bed for days while they recover.

"There's a whole difficulty about that because children have a lot of energy and when you confine them to bed it tends to disrupt their sleeping patterns," he said.

Deep breathing exercises, carried out when playing the game, can help children relax and restore their sleeping patterns. ○

Answering the BIG Question

As you do the following activities, consider the Big Question: **Reading: What's in it for you?**

WRITE TO LEARN Do you think the breath-controlled video game will succeed in its purpose? Will it help children in hospitals relax and sleep better? Write your opinion and supporting reasons in your Learner's Notebook.

LITERATURE GROUPS Talk with two or three students who have read this selection. Imagine what the next steps might be for this research group. Where else could they go with this idea?

A Simple Gift, A Grand Notion

by Tamra Orr
from *The Dawn of Aviation:
The Story of the Wright Brothers*

Can a simple toy inspire two brothers to invent something that changes the world?

Wilbur and Orville looked out the window again. There was still no sign of their father. Would he ever get here?

The brothers, along with their three siblings Katherine, Lorin, and Reuchlin, were used to their father being gone. As the minister for the Church of the United Brethren in Christ, Milton Wright traveled often. He would journey all the way to the west coast to visit other <u>congregations</u>, and although his children missed him, he frequently brought home a toy or other gifts for them. The anticipation of that toy was what kept Wilbur, eleven, and Orville, seven, running to look out the front window. **❶**

Suddenly, there was a sound on the front porch steps. Yes! Father was home. Although he was a stern man, Milton loved his children deeply. Seeing Orville and Wilbur's eager eyes, he pulled out the toy he had hidden behind his back. With a quick flip of the wrist, he sent it flying across the room. The boys were astonished. What had their father given them?

> **❶ Activating Prior Knowledge**
> What do you know about Wilbur and Orville Wright?

"Late in the autumn of 1878," Wilbur recalled in his diaries, "our father came into the house one evening with some object concealed in his hands, and before we could see what it was, he tossed it into the air. Instead of falling to the floor, as we expected, it flew across the room till it struck the ceiling, where it fluttered awhile and finally sank to the floor . . . A toy so delicate lasted only a short time in the hands of small boys, but its memory was abiding."

A quick inspection showed that it was a flying toy called The Bat, made out of thin cork, bamboo, paper, and rubber bands. The boys had heard of this unusual

Vo•cab•u•lary

congregations (kawn gruh GAY shunz) people assembled for church; gatherings

toy. It was an invention of a young Frenchman named Alphonse Penaud. In 1878, everyone was talking about them. The boys immediately began twisting the rubber band and letting the toy fly. Each time, it flew almost fifty feet.

The rest of the evening, as well as the rest of the week and beyond, Orville and Wilbur played with their new flying machine. As toys will do—especially those with paper wings—it broke now and then and each time, the boys repaired it. Using it as a model, they also began building bigger forms. To their disappointment, the bigger ones looked great but would not fly.

"We built a number of copies of this toy," recalled Orville in his diaries, "which flew successfully. But when we undertook to fly the toy on a much larger scale, it failed to work so well. The reason for this was not understood by us at the time, so we finally abandoned the experiment."

No one realized, least of all Orville and Wilbur, that their inability to make the larger toy fly and the mystery behind it would turn into their lives' work and inspiration. From a very simple toy would soon come a truly grand <u>notion</u>. ○

Answering the BIG Question

As you do the following activities, consider the Big Question:
Reading: What's in it for you?

WRITE TO LEARN What would you invent to make the world a better, more efficient, or more enjoyable place? Write about it in a brief entry in your Learner's Notebook. Tell what your invention would do and how it would affect people's lives.

PARTNER TALK Work with a partner who has read this selection. Talk about how different inventions have changed our world. Discuss how the Wright brothers' first successful airplane flight affected people's lives.

Vo•cab•u•lary

notion (NOH shun) an idea, concept, or possibility

My Poems

by Alan Barlow

Who knows what a poem does after it is written?

I am a sun poet
sitting on a ray
of streaming light
writing
gold poems.
Quickly, my poems
shine down on
the earth
and hide
in grains of
burning sand.

I am a rain poet
under an old
gray umbrella
finishing wet, soggy
poems. As I finish,
my poems slowly
run away
and slide in
alleys and streets
of huge cities.

I am a sea poet
riding a sea
turtle while
writing poems.
My poems slither away
and have fun
swimming with fish
in the green, dark
waters.

I am a building poet
on the roof
writing poems.
My poems run into cracks
in walls
and cry out
to me.

I am a space poet
riding on a
falling star.
My poems fly
off
in the cold darkness
and are lost
forever in
twisting mysterious galaxies.

THE PEN
by Muhammad al-Ghuzzi
Tunisia
Translated by May Jayyusi and John Heath-Stubbs

Take a pen in your uncertain fingers.
Trust, and be assured
That the whole world is a sky-blue
butterfly
And words are the nets to
capture it.

Reply to the Question:

"How Can You Become a Poet?"

by Eve Merriam

Can you follow this poet's advice?

take the leaf of a tree
trace its exact shape
the outside edges
and inner lines

memorize the way it is fastened to the twig
(and how the twig arches from the branch)
how it springs forth in April
how it is <u>panoplied</u> in July

by late August
crumple it in your hand
so that you smell its end-of-summer sadness

chew its woody stem

Vo•cab•u•lary

panoplied (PAN uh pleed) brightly colored

listen to its autumn rattle

watch as it <u>atomizes</u> in the November air

then in winter
when there is no leaf left
$\qquad$ invent one ❶ ○

❶ Identifying Author's Purpose
What message about poetry does Eve Merriam want to express?

Answering the BIG Question

As you do the following activities, consider the Big Question:
Reading: What's in it for you?

WRITE TO LEARN Imagine every aspect of a leaf or another natural object. Write a short poem about it in your Learner's Notebook.

PARTNER TALK Join with another student who has read these poems. Talk about which poem you liked best and why.

Vo•cab•u•lary

atomizes (AT uhm yz iz) turns to dust

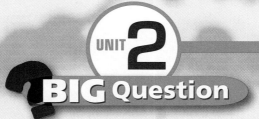

Which is more important—the journey or the destination?

In this unit, you will read about journeys of all kinds. Reading about the different roads people have taken on their life's journey will help you answer for yourself the question: **Which is more important—the journey or the destination?**

Key Reading Skills

As you read the selections in this unit, apply these reading skills.

- **Analyzing** Think about separate parts of a selection in order to understand the entire selection or some part of it.

- **Inferring** Use your reasoning and experiences to figure out things that the author does not say directly.

- **Predicting** Take an educated guess at what will happen in a selection.

- **Comparing and Contrasting** Think about the similarities and differences among characters, events, settings, and other elements of a selection.

The Game

by Walter Dean Myers

In a close game, a good coach knows what makes the difference between a winning team and a losing one.

We had practiced and practiced until it ran out of our ears. Every guy on the team knew every play. We were ready. It meant the championship. Everybody was there. I never saw so many people at the center at one time. We had never seen the other team play but Sam said that he knew some of the players and that they were good. Mr. Reese told us to go out and play as hard as we could every moment we were on the floor. We all shook hands in the locker room and then went out. Mostly we tried to ignore them warming up at the other end of the court but we couldn't help but look a few times. They were doing exactly what we were doing, just shooting a few lay-ups and waiting for the game to begin.

They got the first tap and started passing the ball around. I mean they really started passing the ball around faster than anything I had ever *seen*. Zip! Zip! Zip! Two points! I didn't even know how they could see the ball, let alone get it inside to their big man. We brought the ball down and one of their players stole the ball from Sam. We got back on defense but they weren't in a hurry. The same old thing. Zip! Zip! Zip! Two points! They could pass the ball better than anybody I ever saw. Then we brought the ball down again and Chalky missed a jump shot. He missed the backboard, the rim, everything. One of their players caught the ball and then brought it down and a few seconds later the score was 6–0. We couldn't even get close enough to foul them. Chalky brought the ball down again, passed to Sam cutting across the lane, and Sam walked. They brought the ball down and it was 8–0. **❶**

❶ Comparing and Contrasting How have the two teams performed up to this point?

They were really enjoying the game. You could see. Every time they scored they'd slap hands and carry on. Also, they had some cheerleaders. They had about five girls with little pink skirts on and white sweaters cheering for them.

Clyde brought the ball down this time, passed into our center, a guy named Leon, and Leon turned and missed a hook. They got the <u>rebound</u> and came down, and Chalky missed a steal and fouled his man. That's when Mr. Reese called time out.

"Okay, now, just trade basket for basket. They make a basket, you take your time and you make a basket—don't rush it." Mr. Reese looked at his starting five. "Okay, now, every once in a while take a look over at me and I'll let you know when I want you to make your move. If I put my hands palm down, just keep on playing cool. If I stand up and put my hands up like this"—he put both hands up near his face—"that means to make your move. You understand that?"

Vo•cab•u•lary

rebound (REE bownd) a ball that has bounced off the backboard or rim

The Game

Everyone said that they understood. When the ball was back in play, Chalky and Sam and Leon started setting picks from the outside and then passed to Clyde for our first two points. They got the ball and started passing around again. Zip! Zip! Zip! But this time we were just waiting for that pass underneath and they knew it. Finally they tried a shot from outside and Chalky slapped it away to Sam on the break. We came down real quick and scored. On the way back Mr. Reese showed everybody that his palms were down. To keep playing cool.

They missed their next shot and fouled Chalky. They called time out and, much to my surprise, Mr. Reese put me in. My heart was beating so fast I thought I was going to have a heart attack. Chalky missed the foul shot but Leon slapped the ball out to Clyde, who passed it to me. I dribbled about two steps and threw it back to Leon in the bucket. Then I didn't know what to do so I did what Mr. Reese always told us. If you don't know what to do then, just move around. I started moving toward the corner and then I ran quickly toward the basket. I saw Sam coming at me from the other direction and it was a play. Two guards cutting past and one of the defensive men gets picked off. I ran as close as I could to Sam, and his man got picked off. Chalky threw the ball into him for an easy lay-up. They came down and missed again but one of their men got the rebound in. We brought the ball down and Sam went along the base line for a jump shot, but their center knocked the ball away. I caught it just before it went out at the corner and shot the ball. I remembered what Mr. Reese had said about following your shot in, and I started in after the ball but it went right in. It didn't touch the rim or anything. Swish! ❷

❷ **Inferring**
What is the key to the narrator's success?

One of their players said to watch out for 17—that was me. I played about two minutes more, then Mr. Reese took me out. But I had scored another basket on a lay-up. We were coming back. Chalky and Sam were knocking away just about anything their guards were throwing up, and Leon, Chalky, and Sam controlled the defensive backboard. Mr. Reese brought in Cap, and Cap got fouled two times in two plays. At the end of the half, when I thought we were doing pretty

well, I found out the score was 36–29. They were beating us by seven points. Mr. Reese didn't seem worried, though.

"Okay, everybody, stay cool. No sweat. Just keep it nice and easy."

We came out in the second half and played it pretty cool. Once we came within one point, but then they ran it up to five again. We kept looking over to Mr. Reese to see what he wanted us to do and he would just put his palms down and nod his head for us to play cool. There were six minutes to go when Mr. Reese put me and another guy named Turk in. Now I didn't really understand why he did this because I know I'm not the best basketball player in the world, although I'm not bad, and I know Turk is worse than me. Also, he took out both Sam and Chalky, our two best players. We were still losing by five points, too. And they weren't doing anything wrong. There was a jump ball between Leon and their center when all of a sudden this big cheer goes up and everybody looks over to the sidelines. Well, there

The Game

was Gloria, BB, Maria, Sharon, Kitty, and about four other girls, all dressed in white blouses and black skirts and with big T's on their blouses and they were our cheerleaders. One of their players said something stupid about them but I liked them. They looked real good to me. We controlled the jump and Turk drove right down the lane and made a lay-up. Turk actually made the lay-up. Turk once missed seven lay-ups in a row in practice and no one was even guarding him. But this one he made.

Then one of their men <u>double-dribbled</u> and we got the ball and I passed it to Leon, who threw up a shot and got fouled. The shot went in and when he made the foul shot it added up to a three-point play. They started down court and Mr. Reese started yelling for us to give a foul.

"Foul him! Foul him!" he yelled from the sidelines.

Now this was something we had worked on in practice and that Mr. Reese had told us would only work once in a game. Anybody who plays basketball knows that if you're fouled while shooting the ball you get two foul shots and if you're fouled while not shooting the ball you only get one[1]. So when a guy knows you're going to foul him he'll try to get off a quick shot. **3** At least that's what we hoped. When their guard came across the mid-court line, I ran at him as if I was going to foul him. Then, just as I was going to touch him, I stopped short and moved around him without touching him. Sure enough, he threw the

> **3 Inferring**
> Why will this strategy work only once in a game?

....

[1] The rule about foul shots has changed since this story was written.

Vo•cab•u•lary

double-dribbled (DUH bul DRI buld) made an illegal move in which the player dribbles the ball with both hands or stops and then starts to dribble again

ball wildly toward the basket. It went over the base line and it was our ball. Mr. Reese took me out and Turk and put Sam and Chalky back in. And the game was just about over.

We hadn't realized it but in the two minutes that me and Turk played the score had been tied. When Sam and Chalky came back in they outscored the other team by four points in the last four minutes. We were the champs. We got the first-place trophies and we were so happy we were all jumping around and slapping each other on the back. Gloria and the other girls were just as happy as we were, and when we found that we had an extra trophy we gave it to them. Then Mr. Reese took us all in the locker room and shook each guy's hand and then went out and invited the parents and the girls in. He made a little speech about how he was proud of us and all, and not just because we won tonight but because we had worked so hard to win. When he finished, everybody started clapping for us and, as usual, I started boo-hooing. But it wasn't so bad this time because Leon started boo-hooing worse than me. **4**

We felt so good the next couple of days that it was ridiculous. We'd see someone in the street and we'd just walk up and be happy. Really. ○

4 Analyzing
Why was the narrator's team able to turn the game around and win it?

Answering the
BIG Question

As you do the following activities, consider the Big Question:
Which is more important—the journey or the destination?

WRITE TO LEARN Think about the importance of teamwork in this game. In your Learner's Notebook, write about a time when teamwork allowed you and others to reach a common goal.

LITERATURE GROUPS Meet with two or three other students who have read this selection. Discuss the way the coach called this game. Do you agree that he seemed to value the players' efforts as much as their victory?

TORNADO!

Would you risk your life to unravel the mystery of a tornado?

Storm chasers risk their lives to discover the secrets of these awesome winds.

"One time a tornado we were filming was coming right at us," says filmmaker Sean Casey. "When you jump out of the truck to get the shot, anything can happen. As it moved closer, the wind picked up, and we felt as if the wind were pulling us into the tornado.

"The trick is knowing when to get out of there," says Casey. With swirling winds that can top 300 miles (483 kilometers) an hour, twisters can rip up trees, turn houses into piles of twisted wood, and toss cars around like toys. They're nature's most violent nasty storms.

Casey and his crew always have to be ready to run. "We're out there filming," Casey says. "But the truck motor's running and the doors are all wide open." If the storm gets too close, they throw their equipment in the truck and tear out of there—fast. ❶

People like Casey chase tornadoes to make large-format films. But to find the storms, Casey tags along with a group of meteorologists, or weather scientists, who chase storms to find out why tornadoes form in some thunderstorms but not in others. The data that storm-chasing meteorologists collect could make it easier to predict which storms will produce tornadoes. That, says storm chaser and scientist Herb Stein, could help meteorologists warn people in the path of a storm to take shelter before it hits.

❶ Analyzing
What is the difference between taking a reasonable risk and being reckless?

Casey's team of filmmakers and the team of scientists Stein works with have had close calls. "We were following a storm one day and we heard the meteorologists say on the truck radio there was a tornado right where we were," says Casey. "But the rain was pouring down so hard and the wind was howling so much that we couldn't see it. It was like being in this dark cloud with a monster, but we couldn't tell where the monster was."

Stein remembers that storm, too. "As the wind picked up and visibility dropped to zero, we were forced to stop in the road. The wind pushed our 13-ton (13,209-kilogram) radar truck backward. Suddenly—*whump!* Debris hit the side of the vehicle as the truck made strange groaning noises caused by the 100-mile (161-kilometer)-an-hour winds. After it was over we saw telephone poles bent over by the winds."

The chase has its exciting moments. But it can also be long and <u>tedious</u>. "A lot of people see storm chasers on TV or in movies like *Twister* and they think storm chasing is very exciting," says Stein. "It's nothing like that. We might drive 10,000 miles (16,093 kilometers) in a six- to eight-week season

Vo•cab•u•lary

tedious (TEE dee us) tiresome; boring

This is what remained of Evelyn's Antiques in Spencer, South Dakota.

and see one tornado that lasts a few minutes."

"To keep at it, storm chasing has to be a real passion for us," Casey says. ❷

> ❷ **Analyzing** Why are storm chasers so passionate about this risky job?

For the scientists, it's also an important mission. Stein remembers a killer tornado that hit tiny Spencer, South Dakota, in 1998. "It wiped that town off the map," says Stein. "That kind of thing really makes you remember why you do this." Seeing a tornado up close is exciting. But what's even more important is that storm chasers gain insight about twisters that could one day save lives. ○

Answering the BIG Question

As you do the following activities, consider the Big Question:
Which is more important—the journey or the destination?

WRITE TO LEARN Consider how the filmmakers and storm chasers work together to gather information about tornadoes. Write an entry in your Learner's Notebook about another example of how people work together to get a job done.

LITERATURE GROUPS Get together with two or three other students who have read this selection. Discuss the risks that are a part of various jobs. Talk about why people are willing to take these risks.

DRUMBEATS AND BULLETS

by Jim Murphy

Imagine you are twelve years old, maybe thirteen, and you are writing a letter home—from a battlefield.

The groggy soldier woke up to a persistent, brain-rattling drumming noise. *Thrump. Thrump. Thrump.* He rolled over in an attempt to ignore the sound and pulled his blanket up over his head. The drumming went on and intensified as drummers all over camp signaled the call to <u>muster</u>. There was no escaping it, and eventually—and usually with a grumble—the soldier got up to start another day.

Vo·cab·u·lary

muster (MUH stur) to bring together a group of soldiers for a particular reason—for example, to march or for inspection

Drumbeats and Bullets

Soldiers probably came to hate the sound of the drums, especially when they heard them on a drizzly, cold morning. Yet drummer boys who served during the Civil War provided valuable service to the armies of both sides, although some didn't realize it at first.

"I wanted to fight the Rebs," a twelve-year-old boy wrote, "but I was very small and they would not give me a musket. The next day I went back and the man behind the desk said I looked as if I could hold a drum and if I wanted I could join that way. I did, but I was not happy to change a musket for a stick."

This boy was disappointed at being assigned a "nonfighting" and, to him, dull job. Most likely, he saw himself always drumming in parades or in the safety of camp. He would soon learn differently.

The beat of the drum was one of the most important means of communicating orders to soldiers in the Civil War. Drummers did find themselves in camp sounding the routine calls to muster or meals and providing the beat for marching drills. But more often than not, they were with the troops in the field, not just marching to the site of the battle but in the middle of the fighting. It was the drumbeat that told the soldiers how and when to maneuver as smoke poured over the battlefield. And the sight of a drummer boy showed soldiers where their unit was located, helping to keep them close together.

Drummers were such a vital part of battle communication that they often found themselves the target of enemy fire. "A ball hit my drum and bounced off and I fell over," a Confederate drummer at the Battle of Cedar Creek recalled. "When I got up, another ball tore a hole in the drum and another came so close to my ear that I heard it sing." ❶

Naturally, such killing fire alarmed many drummer boys at first. But like their counterparts with rifles, they soon learned how to face enemy shells without flinching. Fourteen-year-old Orion Howe was struck by

> ❶ **Comparing and Contrasting**
> How did a drummer's life differ from what the boy had imagined?

several Confederate bullets during the Battle of Vicksburg in 1863. Despite his wounds, he maintained his position and relayed the orders given him. For his bravery, Howe would later receive the Medal of Honor.

Drumming wasn't the only thing these boys did, either. While in camp, they would carry water, rub down horses, gather wood, or cook for the soldiers. There is even evidence that one was a barber for the troops when he wasn't drumming. After a battle, most drummers helped carry wounded soldiers off the field or assisted in burial details[1]. And many drummer boys even got their wish to fight the enemy.

Fighting in the Civil War was particularly bloody. Of the 900 men in the First Maine Heavy Artillery, 635 became casualties *in just seven minutes* of fighting at the Battle of Petersburg. A North Carolina regiment saw 714 of its 800 soldiers killed at Gettysburg. At such a time, these boys put down their drums and took up whatever rifle was handy. One such drummer was Johnny Clem.

Clem ran away from home in 1861 when he was eleven years old. He enlisted, and the Twenty-second Michigan Regiment took him in as their drummer, paying him thirteen dollars a month for his services. Several months later, at the Battle of Shiloh, Clem earned the nickname of "Johnny Shiloh" when a piece of cannon shell bounced off a tree stump and destroyed his drum. When another drum was shattered in battle, Clem found a musket and fought bravely for the rest of the war, becoming a sergeant in the fall of 1863. ❷

❷ **Analyzing**
Why was it so important for drummer boys to be adaptable?

....
[1] Here, *details* refers to persons or groups selected for a particular task.

Drumbeats and Bullets

The Civil War would be the last time drummer boys would be used in battle. The roar of big cannons and <u>mortars</u>, the rapid firing of thousands of rifles, and the shouts of tens of thousands of men made hearing a drumbeat difficult. More and more, bugles were being used to pass along orders. Military tactics were changing, too. Improved weapons made it impractical to have precise lines of soldiers face their enemy at close range. Instead, smaller, fast-moving units and trench warfare, neither of which required drummers, became popular.

Even as their role in the fighting was changing, Civil War drummers stayed at their positions signaling orders to the troops. Hundreds were killed and thousands more wounded. "A cannon ball came bouncing across the cornfield," a drummer boy recalled, "kicking up dirt and dust each time it struck the earth. Many of the men in our company took shelter behind a stone wall, but I stood where I was and never stopped drumming. An officer came by on horseback and chastised the men, saying 'this boy puts you to shame. Get up and move forward.' We all began moving across the cornfield . . . Even when the fighting was at its fiercest and I was frightened, I stood straight and did as I was

Answering the BIG Question

As you do the following activities, consider the Big Question:
Which is more important—the journey or the destination?

WRITE TO LEARN Think about why these young boys wanted to go to war. Write a brief entry in your Learner's Notebook about what you might have done in their situation.

PARTNER TALK Meet with a classmate who has read this selection. Discuss whether the drummer boys should have been allowed to take up arms against the enemy. Give reasons to support your opinions.

Vo·cab·u·lary

mortars (MOR turz) cannons with a short and wide barrel that fire shells at a high angle over a short distance

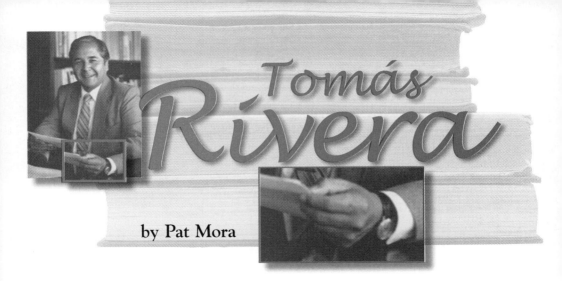

Tomás Rivera

by Pat Mora

A great man is remembered for what he did for others after raising himself from poverty.

They knew so much, his hands
spoke of the journey from Crystal City
to Iowa, Michigan, Minnesota, year after year
dirt-dusted in fields and orchards,
his hands a pillow at night,
in bare, cold buildings,
family laughter his favorite blanket.

On slow days his hands
gathered books at city dumps,
saved like the memories of smiling
hard at that first grade teacher
and her noises in the other language
that didn't laugh like Spanish.

Those hands clenched in the dark
at _víboras_, _víboras_ hissing
  we don't want you, you people have lice
as the school door slammed
but Tomás learned,

Vo•cab•u•lary

víboras (BEE boh rahs) snakes (Spanish)

79

and his hands began to hold books
gently, with affection. ❶ He searched
for stories about his people and finally
gave their words sound, wrote the books
he didn't have, we didn't have.

❶ **Predicting**
How will books change the course of Tomás Rivera's journey?

And he graduated over and over
until one day he was <u>Chancellor</u> Rivera,
famous Chicano, too needed,
his hands too full of us
to sit alone and write green stories
alive with voices, "fiesta of the living,"
pressing, the present pressing
like the hands reaching out to him,
and he'd hug the small, brown hands,
his hands whispering his secret
learn, learn
his face a wink, teasing out their smiles,
a face all could rest in,
like the cherries he picked, dark,
sweet, round a pit, tooth-breaker
for the unwary, the lazy, the cruel.

His hands knew about the harvest,
tasted the laborer's sweat in the sweet
cantaloupes he sliced, knew how to use
laughter to remove stubborn roots
of bitter weeds: prejudice, indifference,
the boy from Crystal City, Texas,
not a legend to be shelved,
but a man whose <u>*abrazos*</u> still warm
us yet say, "Now you."

Vo•cab•u•lary

chancellor (CHAN suh lur) head of a university; Tomás Rivera was chancellor of the University of California, Riverside.
abrazos (ah BRAH sos) hugs; embraces (Spanish)

By Accident

by Jane O. Wayne

Does love see in black and white, or is it color blind?

Because I brought him here
I hold his hand
while the surgeon cleans his leg,
a boy I hardly know, a child
my daughter's age. Years ago
a black nurse held
my white hand in a hospital and I
squeezed then just as he does now
a stranger never thanked
never forgotten.

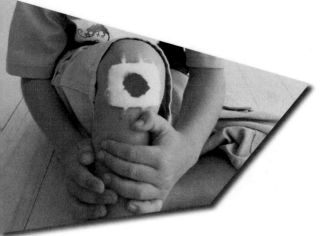

I know how it happens,
how pain softens us as easily
as habit hardens, how
we meet now and if we meet again
we both avert our eyes,
the boy and I,
as from the gash itself,
the white seams gaping on the raw red,
we turn away. Often I think we can,
given half a chance, love anyone. ❷ ○

> ❷ **Inferring**
> What does the speaker seem to suggest about racial prejudice?

Answering the BIG Question

As you do the following activities, consider the Big Question:
Which is more important—the journey or the destination?

WRITE TO LEARN Think about how racial prejudice affected the life of Tomás Rivera. Then write a brief entry in your Learner's Notebook about an incident involving prejudice that you have experienced or witnessed.

PARTNER TALK Meet with a partner who has read these poems. Discuss how in the poem "By Accident," race seems unimportant in a time of crisis. Then talk about how racial barriers often break down, at least temporarily, when natural disasters strike.

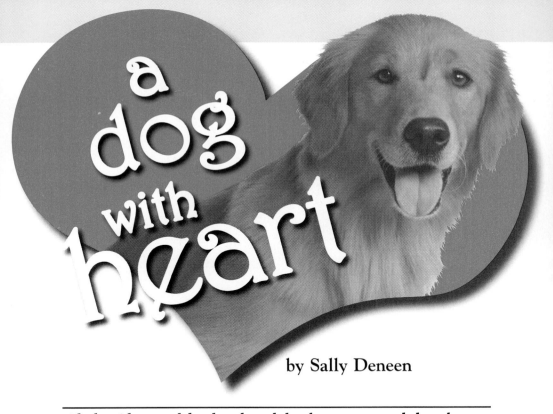

a dog with heart

by Sally Deneen

Find out how a sick, abandoned dog became a much-loved helper to dozens of people.

The phone rang at about 4:00 P.M., and Suzanne Rider picked up the handset to hear an animal control employee tell her: "We've picked up a homeless Golden Retriever with <u>heartworms</u>. If you don't take him, he will be PTS." Rider knew what PTS meant: put to sleep.

She quickly drove to see the dog before closing time. As the west coast coordinator for Golden Retriever Rescue of Mid-Florida, she knew that this particular pound provided short notice.

Vo•cab•u•lary

heartworms (HART wurmz) parasitic worms that live in the heart vessels of dogs. Left untreated, heartworm infestation is fatal.

A Dog with Heart

Rider walked through the door and saw him—the first dog in the first cage: a quiet, thin, timid, one-year-old retriever.

"When I walked over to his cage, his tail started wagging," recalls Rider, who, with husband Tony, has fostered nearly 120 dogs through the years at their home in Lutz, Florida, near Tampa. "He was looking through the chain-link cage and snuggled his face against my hand. Right then, I decided I had to save this one."

But soon after the pooch got to her home in February 2002, he began to feel the effects of his first treatment for heartworms. "He was throwing up almost hourly and having trouble breathing," Rider says. "A couple days into the treatment, I thought we were going to lose him."

But the <u>stoic</u> dog, nicknamed JD, didn't fret despite obvious discomfort.

"Heartworm treatment is generally successful in medium

Vo•cab•u•lary
stoic (STOH ik) showing patience and endurance in a difficult situation

to large dogs, especially when they are young and otherwise healthy," explains Guy Hancock, DVM, M.Ed., president of the Florida Animal Health Foundation and dean of the School of Veterinary Technology at St. Petersburg College in St. Petersburg, Florida. But, he points out, "The difficulties with heartworm treatment are many. It is expensive, and the outcome is uncertain due to not knowing how many worms the dog harbors." Among other things, complications can be serious or fatal.

Two weeks passed, and JD seemed to feel better.

He started walking around the house after three and a half weeks. Antsy, he barked as if to say he wanted to play outside with the other dogs. Still undergoing heartworm treatment, though, he needed to avoid strenuous exercise. So, JD and Rider went off to obedience class to exercise his mind and gain his Canine Good Citizen status. New and improved, the now-healthy dog ended his two months' stay with Rider and moved to a neighboring county to a permanent home and a new name— Keegan.

"Keegan walked into the house and went straight into the pool," says adoring owner Sue Keiser, of Palm Harbor. "It was like he had always been here."

Keiser began taking the retriever to retirement homes and hospitals upon graduation from an advanced obedience class. Retirees soon began to wait in the lobby to see Keegan and other rescued retrievers the minute they walked through the door at Royal Palms of Largo, says Dee Ragan, lifestyles director. More than 200 seniors over age 70 live independently at Royal Palms, where brochures, fliers, and a public-address announcement alert residents to the dogs' very popular visits. "I would put it right up there with bridge. And that's big," Ragan says.

"When they touch the animal and the animal gives them love back . . . it's definitely therapy," she adds. ❶

❶ Comparing and Contrasting
How has Keegan's life changed since Rider rescued him from the pound?

A Dog with Heart

In 2004 Keegan entered the Florida Animal Hall of Fame. His rags-to-riches story and pet therapy work earned him the honor at a Tampa ceremony. "We were all hooting and hollering and clapping and screaming," Rider says.

"We were impressed with Keegan's therapy work and his suitability to it," says Dr. Hancock, an FAHF member. "He illustrates why society should care about reducing the number of homeless pets, and the value that animals can bring to our lives that we so often under-appreciate."

As proud foster mom Rider sees it, now four-year-old Keegan went from "someone's disposable pet to someone's lifelong dream." ○

Answering the BIG Question

As you do the following activities, consider the Big Question:
Which is more important—the journey or the destination?

WRITE TO LEARN Think about how Keegan fought to regain his health. Then write an entry in your Learner's Notebook about a time you had to struggle to get something you really wanted.

PARTNER TALK With a partner, discuss the role Suzanne Rider played in Keegan's recovery. Then talk about how we often need the help of others as we journey toward a desired destination.

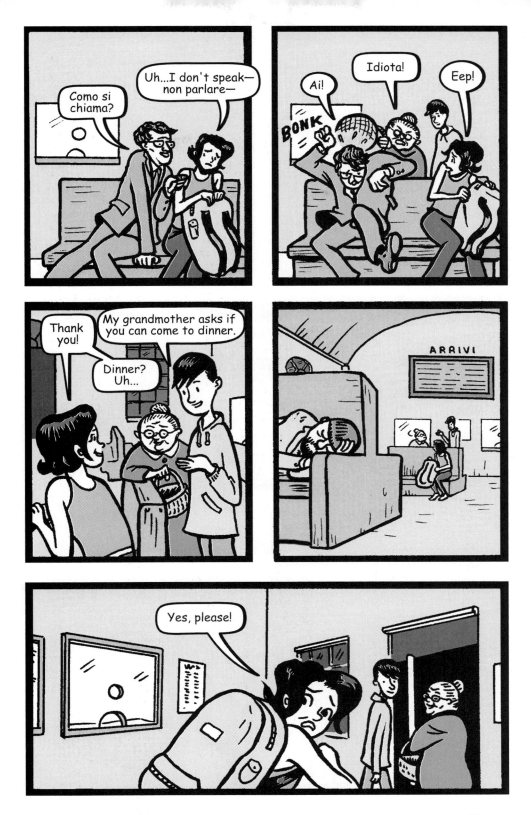

WRITE TO LEARN
Think about the goal Tina set out to achieve and what actually happened. In your Learner's Notebook, write about the ways in which Tina's detour made her experience better.

Soap Box Derby

Puts Kids' Creativity, Racing Skills to the Test

Read about kids who build their own vehicles and race to the finish line with no brakes.

Imagine racing downhill, pulled by <u>gravity</u> alone, in a small vehicle with no brakes. That's exactly what 500 kids did recently in the 68th annual All-American Soap Box Derby. Kids ages nine to sixteen traveled to Akron, Ohio, for the race.

The kids raced in soap box carts that they built either from scratch or using kits. Soap box carts can fit only one person, the

---

Vo•cab•u•lary

gravity (GRAV ih tee) the pull that the Earth exerts on objects on or near its surface

driver, and are steered by a wheel or even a rope wrapped around the tires of the cart. **❶**

The Soap Box Derby races are divided into various levels of competition and skill. Sixteen-year-old Stephanie Inglezakis won the 2005 Master's Division in a cart that took her and her grandfather six months to build. "I didn't expect to win," Stephanie told the *Akron Beacon Journal*. "Then I crossed the finish line, and they're all running to me and giving me hugs." Stephanie received a $5,000 scholarship for winning the race.

The All-American Soap Box Derby began in 1934. Back then, carts were made out of orange crates, sheet metal, and baby stroller wheels. Today, the carts are a little more advanced thanks to better materials, easy-to-use kits, and creative themes. ○

❶ Inferring
What type of kid might want to build a car and race in this national derby?

Answering the BIG Question

As you do the following activities, consider the Big Question:
Which is more important—the journey or the destination?

WRITE TO LEARN Imagine you are thinking of entering the Soap Box Derby. What interests you more—building your vehicle or racing it? Why? Write your thoughts in a brief entry in your Learner's Notebook.

LITERATURE GROUPS Meet with two or three other students who have read this selection. Discuss the importance of preparing for a competition, such as a race. Then talk about preparation as an important part of the journey toward a goal.

Vo•cab•u•lary

scholarship (SKAWL ur ship) money awarded to a student for education

THE END OF THE WORLD

by Jenny Leading Cloud

In a hidden cave you will never find, an old woman controls the end of the world—or does she?

Somewhere, at a place where the prairie and the Mako Sica, the <u>badlands</u>, meet, there is a hidden cave. Not for many generations has anyone been able to find it. Even now, with so many cars and highways and tourists, no one has found this cave.

In the cave lives an old woman. She is so old that her face looks like a shriveled-up walnut. She is dressed in rawhide, the way people used to go around before the white people came to this country. She is sitting there—has been sitting there for a thousand years or more—working on a blanket strip for her buffalo robe. She is making that blanket strip out of dyed porcupine quills, the way our ancestors did before white traders brought glass beads to this turtle continent. Resting beside her, licking his paws, watching her all the time, is a Shunka Sapa, a huge black dog. His eyes never wander from the old woman whose teeth are worn flat, worn down to little stumps from using them to flatten numberless porcupine quills.

Vo•cab•u•lary

badlands (BAD landz) a dry region with little plant life

The End of the World

A few steps from where the old woman sits working on her blanket strip, a big fire is kept going. She lit this fire a thousand or more years ago and has kept it alive ever since. Over the fire hangs a big earthenware pot, the kind some Indian people used to make before the white man came with his kettles of iron. Inside the big pot, wojapi is boiling and bubbling. Wojapi is berry soup. It is good and sweet and red. That wojapi has been boiling in that pot for a long time, ever since the fire was lit.

Every now and then the old woman gets up to stir the wojapi in the huge earthenware pot. She is so old and <u>feeble</u> that it takes her a while to get up and hobble over to the fire. The moment the old woman's back is turned, the huge, black dog starts pulling out the porcupine quills from her blanket strip. This way, she never makes any progress, and her quillwork remains forever half finished. The Sioux people used to say that if the woman ever finished her blanket strip, in the very moment that she would thread the last porcupine quill to complete her design, the world would come to an end. **1** ○

1 Analyzing
What does this story explain about the world?

Answering the BIG Question

As you do the following activities, consider the Big Question:
Which is more important—the journey or the destination?

WRITE TO LEARN Think about how the black dog delays the end of the world in this legend. In your Learner's Notebook, write about a time when you tried to delay the end of a journey.

PARTNER TALK Discuss with a partner the saying "All good things must come to an end." Does the saying apply to this legend? Why or why not?

Vo•cab•u•lary

feeble (FEE bul) weak; without strength

Smoke **Signals**

by Eva Chen

Read stories of teens who have taken a journey they wish they'd passed up.

Smoke Signals

Tami still remembers the first time she lit up. A fourteen-year-old eighth-grader, she was dating a high school freshman. "I smoked because I thought it would impress him. I never thought I'd get addicted," says Tami, an Ohio native. Five years later, she is still smoking.

> "I never thought I'd get addicted."

A former athlete from upstate New York with multiple sports medals, Alexis also had her first cigarette when she was fourteen. "My best friend's brother was older and was a total bad boy, into drugs, drinking, and other stuff," she says. Under his influence, she picked up a Newport menthol cigarette. Eight years later, she is still smoking (and the aforementioned "bad boy" brother is in prison).

Amanda, nineteen, had her first cigarette last year in an attempt to fit in. "My friends all smoke. I hated it but I felt like I either had to join in or not be friends with them," she says. "So I had my first cigarette during finals. It was terrible—I got dizzy, my stomach ached, and I coughed. But I learned to get used to it. And now I can't go a day without smoking."

Every day, more than 4,400 teens try a cigarette for the first time. Most know the risks of smoking—like Amanda, they've gone through the rote high school health-ed class in which images of tobacco-blackened lungs and tar-stained teeth are displayed on the blackboard. "But something is clearly lost in translation," says Thomas Glynn, Ph.D., director of cancer science and trends at the American Cancer Society in Washington, D.C. "Ninety percent of all smokers started smoking as teenagers. ❶ And because much of the damage isn't immediately visible, it seems harmless. 'Seems' being the operative word."

However, some short-term effects are

> **❶ Inferring**
> Why do you think that relatively few people start smoking after their teen years?

hard to miss. "Whenever I go to the dentist, they always ask about my smoking," says Tami. "I didn't realize people could tell I was a smoker just from my teeth." Alexis finds that she must constantly cough and clear her throat "like an old man." In addition to the wheezing and stained teeth, smoking has been linked to premature wrinkles, cataracts, tooth loss, excess phlegm, and weight gain (to name just a few). Contrary to popular belief, smoking doesn't help you lose weight—in fact, one study shows that female smokers end up having a more masculine pattern of body-fat distribution. Smokers also get sick more easily and more often than non-smokers, and may have trouble keeping up with non-smoking friends in gym class. "If you start smoking when you're a teen, you impair the development of your lungs," warns David Kamelhar, M.D., a pulmonologist and clinical associate professor of medicine at NYU School of Medicine in New York City. Adds Glynn, "You won't be able to do sports as well, sing as well, or do anything active as

> In addition to the wheezing and stained teeth, smoking has been linked to premature wrinkles, cataracts, tooth loss, excess phlegm, and weight gain...

Vo•cab•u•lary

cataracts (KAT uh rakts) an eye disease in which the lens becomes cloudy and which results in total blindness if not treated
pulmonologist (pul mun AH luh jist) a medical doctor specializing in treatment of the lungs and lung disease

well—you'll be playing catch-up for the rest of your life." This is an experience all too familiar to Alexis. "I used to ice-skate six hours a day, I was on the cross-country team, I played lacrosse, soccer, basketball—you name it," she says. "Then I started smoking. I wish I was the athletic girl I used to be." ❷

❷ **Comparing and Contrasting** In what ways are teens who smoke different from those who don't?

Most worryingly, smoking is a direct cause of lung cancer, making you fifteen times more likely to develop the typically fatal disease. Anyone who thinks that lung cancer is a problem for "old people" (as Tami puts it) should talk to Susan Levine. "My daughter started smoking when she was twelve and was always out of breath as she got older," says Levine, who owns a modeling agency in New York City. "We always thought she had allergies or that she was just working too hard. When she was twenty-five we found out she had lung cancer. She died less than three years later."

Many teens start smoking under the belief that they'll quit before they cause long-term damage. The actual facts? If you're a smoker, even if you quit two days, two months, or two years from now, you'll have an elevated risk of lung cancer for the rest of your life. And statistics show that more than five million people under eighteen who currently smoke will eventually die from a smoking-related disease.

The future isn't entirely bleak for reformed smokers though. "The human body can bounce back," says Glynn. "Function won't return to 100 percent but, after a few years, it will be close to that." One report from the U.S. Surgeon General says that many of the negative side effects of

...five million people under eighteen who currently smoke will eventually die from a smoking-related disease.

smoking (shortness of breath, coughing, heartbeat irregularities) go away within a few months of quitting.

Alexis has tried to quit seven times, including once, semi-successfully, by using lollipops. "I got so many cavities and eventually went back to smoking," she says. "I'm on the patch now." Her struggle is not atypical. According to a recent study, nearly three out of four smokers want to cease smoking, have tried to do so, and have failed. Not surprising, since the success rate of quitting smoking is staggeringly low: five percent. Amanda is still trying to quit. "It's like I chose this stupid path and now it's going to kill me," she says. "I think about that all the time. I'll be paying for my bad decision." Lisa Abroms Herz, a licensed social worker and the clinical director of adolescent programs at the Freedom Institute (a private drug treatment center in California), believes that nicotine is one of the most addictive substances. "People are always shocked when I use the word 'drug' in conjunction with tobacco," she says. "But that's what it is. It's as addictive as heroin, alcohol, cocaine, and pot."

Don't be fooled by the lure of "light" cigarettes. "Light cigarettes are as addictive as full-strength," says Glynn. "They contain ammonia—yes, the household cleaner—which makes nicotine easier to absorb. So while there may be less nicotine, it's easier for the body to access."

The best way to not get hooked? Don't start (one study from the University of California at Irvine showed that all you need is one brief exposure to nicotine to get addicted). Take Emily's example: "Some people think smoking looks glamorous," she says. "But it doesn't appeal to me. The problems it comes with—parents being disappointed, getting sick, teeth turning yellow—are anything but cool."

Smoking turns teeth yellow.

Glenda, a twenty-year-old from Maryland, got her wake-up call when a family member passed away. "My grandfather died of lung cancer and it made me stop being a social smoker," she says. "To be honest, I never really liked it in the first place. I don't know why I did it."

As for Tami, she still believes that smoking is just something she'll grow out of. "Even though I've been smoking for five years, I just don't think this phase will last," she explains. "Time goes by so quickly, but I feel immortal. I'm only nineteen. I have some time." **3** A thought shared by most smokers—until it's too late. ○

3 Analyzing
Do you think Tami will grow out of smoking? Why or why not?

Answering the BIG Question

As you do the following activities, consider the Big Question:
Which is more important—the journey or the destination?

WRITE TO LEARN Think about the ways in which the teens interviewed for this article became addicted to nicotine. Then think about another time when taking one small step can start a person on a long journey. Write about it in your Learner's Notebook.

PARTNER TALK Discuss with a partner the journey that smokers begin with their first cigarette. Most often, the destination is a lifelong addiction to nicotine. Is any part of the journey worth the destination? Why or why not?

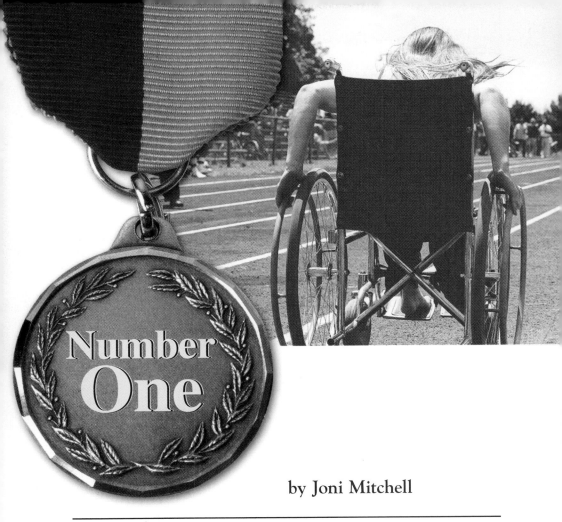

Number One

by Joni Mitchell

When you've got it all, will you be truly happy?

Got to be a winner—trophy winner
Get to hold your head up high up!
Number One!

Got to be a winner—trophy winner
Get to hold your head up high up!
Number One!

Number One
Number One
Honey tell me—

When your working day is done—
Were you reaching for the high rung—
Reaching to be number one?

You get a car
You want a boat
You want an eenie-meenie-miney miney-moe.
Oh there must be more to living
Than a <u>mortgage</u> and a lawn to mow.

Sweaty work
And lucky breaks
And blood and tears is all it takes
To be a winner!
People cheer
And people gasp
People want your autograph
When you're a winner!

Win and lose
Win and lose
To the loser go the heartsick blues.
To the victor goes the spoiling
Honey—did you win or lose?

Sweaty work
Lucky breaks
Blood and tears is all it takes to be a winner!
People cheer
People gasp
People want your autograph
When you're a winner!

Run, run, run, run
Let's see you run
We'll be betting by the starting gun!
Shall we shower you with flowers

Vo·cab·u·lary

mortgage (MOR gij) a loan on a house or property

Or shall we shun ya
When your race is run?
Will we shower you with flowers
Or will we shun ya
When your race is run?

Got to be a winner—trophy winner!
Get to hold your head up high up!
Number One! **1** ○

1 Analyzing
What message about winning do you think the songwriter wants to share?

Singer–songwriter
Joni Mitchell
poses with the
Century Award.

Answering the BIG Question

As you do the following activities, consider the Big Question:
Which is more important—the journey or the destination?

WRITE TO LEARN Think about a time when you achieved something through hard work, good luck, or both. Was it everything you had hoped for? Write about the experience in your Learner's Notebook.

LITERATURE GROUPS Meet with several students who have read this selection. Discuss these questions: Do most "winners" enjoy the journey as much as the destination? Are most of them happy once they reach their goal?

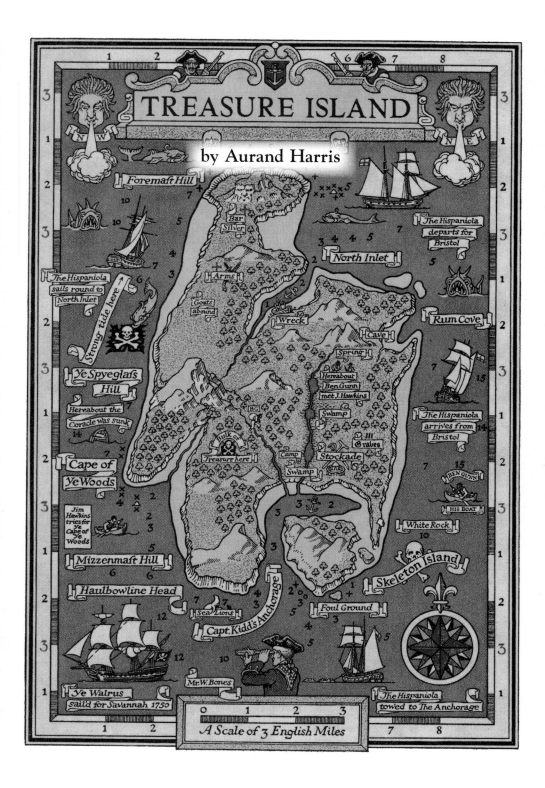

TREASURE ISLAND

by Aurand Harris

The year is 1750. There's action aplenty, with a young boy, bloodthirsty pirates, a sea chest, an island map marked with X's, and . . . buried treasure, of course!

Characters

Mrs. Hawkins

Jim Hawkins

Billy Bones

Dogger

Blind Pew

Dirk

Black Dog

Doctor Livesey

Squire Trelawney

Time

The year 1750.

Setting

England, at the Admiral Benbow Inn, on the dock at Bristol.

Scene 1

The curtain of the Toy Theatre rises. The scene is the interior of the Admiral Benbow Inn, England, 1750.

Mrs. Hawkins. *(enters* UL. *Music dims out.)* Jim? Jim Hawkins! There's much to do. Bring up another keg of ale—Jim? *(comes downstage, outside "house")* Here you are. Always outside looking at the sea. I heard the stagecoach go by. We'll hope it brings a traveler. We could use another lodger at the Admiral Benbow Inn. Here, put on your apron.

Vo•cab•u•lary

UL stage direction "upstage left." DL is "downstage left," UR is "upstage right," and so on.

Jim. (*takes apron, puzzled*) Apron?

Mrs. Hawkins. Now be about your work. Draw some water and come into the dining room and lay the table for tea. (*exits into "house"*)

Jim. Wear an apron? Set the table for tea? Where are the pirates? The buried treasure? I thought I'd meet a fierce, fighting <u>buccaneer</u>. A terrifying robber of the sea! (Billy Bones *enters L, fulfilling* Jim's *description of him.*) With a pistol at his belt, and a cutlass at his side, a patch over his eye, and a voice like a clap of thunder.

Bones. (*Shouts.*) BOY! (Jim *jumps in fright.*) Be this the Admiral Benbow Inn? (Jim *nods.*) Aye, it's a handy cove, and has a good view of the sea. Be there many lodgers inside? (*louder*) I asked you, mate, if the rooms be filled with lodgers? (Jim *shakes his head.*) Then this is the place for me. (*calls off L*) Here you, bring up alongside the chest. (Dogger, *a villager, enters L, carrying a small sea chest.*) I'll be lodging here. Put it down inside.

Dogger. Yes, sir. (*carrying the chest into "house," he stumbles.* Bones *holds him by the collar.*)

Bones. Easy, matey! That sea chest is all I have. Give it a care!

Dogger. Safe it will be, sir, inside. (*exits UL*)

Bones. You, lad, can you not speak? (Jim *nods.*) Then pipe up. Give us a wag of your tongue.

Jim. Yes, sir.

Bones. You can call me "Captain."

Jim. Yes, sir. Captain.

Bones. The great thing with boys is discipline. If you be the serving boy, wear your apron.

Jim. But I . . .

Vo•cab•u•lary

buccaneer (buk kuh NEER) a pirate; outlaw of the sea

Bones. Your apron—on! Before I raise my voice and my cutlass! Discipline, that's what you learn on my ship! (Jim *quickly puts on apron.*) I'll have a sit inside and a bottle of rum.

Jim. Rum?

Bones. Aye, lad, I'll tell you rum is my best mate. I been places hot as pitch, men dropping dead with Yellow Jack, and I lived on rum.

Jim. You've sailed in ships?

Bones. Aye, the stories I could tell. But I'm not talking. (*tosses a coin in the air*) See that? A silver fourpenny. It's yours—

Jim. (*grabs for it*) Mine?

Bones. —if—you keep your eyes open and tell me if any seafaring men be coming along. And mark ye, be on the lookout for the worst one. He's only got one leg.

Jim. One leg?

Bones. One leg—and a peg one. (*exits into "house,"[1] UL, calling*) Rum! I'm wanting a bottle of rum!

Jim. (*excited, speaks to audience*) He looks like a pirate.

Bones. (*offstage, sings*) "Fifteen men on a dead man's chest, Yo-ho-ho, and a bottle of rum—"

Jim. He sounds like a pirate! ❶

❶ Comparing and Contrasting How does Billy Bones compare to Jim's idea of a pirate?

Bones. (*offstage, sings*) "Drink and the Devil has done for the rest, Yo-ho-ho, and a bottle of rum."

Jim. I think he is a pirate! (*Music of "Yo-ho-ho" plays loudly, as* Jim *happily pantomimes dueling, excitedly slashing with imaginary cutlass. He gives a final happy "yo-ho-ho!" and exits DR. Music reaches a climax for the end of the scene.*)

....

[1] "House" refers to a part of the set painted to represent a house.

Scene 2

(the same. Mrs. Hawkins enters DL. She wears a hat and shawl. She enters "house," talking toward L, where she thinks Jim is, and hangs her hat and shawl in the closet which is at R.)

Fifteen men on a dead man's chest,
Yo-ho-ho, and a bottle of rum—
Drink and the Devil has done for the rest,
Yo-ho-ho, and a bottle of rum.

Mrs. Hawkins. I'm back, Jim. All the village is talking about the Captain. And after last night. Falling on the floor like he did! Heart attack. Yes, and too much rum. Rum will be the death of him, all right. Well, I've sent for Dr. Livesey. I am not going to let the Captain die before he pays me for his lodging. Jim? Where are you?

Jim. *(offstage)* Up here.

Mrs. Hawkins. Every day he sits, watches every ship in the cove, every man that goes by. He's done something wicked, I'll wager, and his evil deeds are about to catch up with him. Jim! Where are you?

Jim. *(offstage)* Coming down.

Mrs. Hawkins. Down? Where?

Jim. *(jumps to floor and crawls out of fireplace)* In the fireplace.

Mrs. Hawkins. Jim, what have you been up to?

Jim. I've been up to the top! Climbed the pegs in the chimney and saved a bird's nest.

Mrs. Hawkins. *(takes bird's nest)* Let me have it. Now, Jim, you must keep the Captain quiet until the doctor comes. I want no more heart attacks. And no more rum. Listen. Someone is coming up the road. See who it is. *(She exits UR. Jim comes out of "house," looks DL.)*

Jim. It's a blind man.

Pew. (Blind Pew *is heard tapping his cane off DL. He enters, a dreadful looking figure, tapping his way toward the inn.*) Will any kind friend inform a poor blind man who lost the sight of his eyes defending England, where or in what part of this country he may now be?

Jim. You are in front of the Admiral Benbow Inn.

Pew. I hear a voice, a young voice. Come. Stand closer. Is this the inn where Billy Bones lives?

Jim. There is one here who calls himself "Captain."

Pew. Would he have a cut on his right cheek and a patch on his left eye?

Jim. Yes.

Pew. He's the same! (*cackles with a laugh*) We're going to give Bill a little surprise. Now lend me your hand and lead me in.

Jim. (Pew *feels for* Jim's *hand, then suddenly grips it, twisting* Jim's *arm behind him.*) Oh!

Pew. (*with menace and cruelty*) Now, boy, take me in to the captain. Or I'll break your arm. March. (*Raises his cane to strike.*) Which way? (Jim, *in pain, leads* Pew *into "house."*) Call him to come out.

Jim. Captain. Captain, sir.

Bones. (*offstage*) Aye! Who calls?

Pew. When he comes in the room, you cry out, "Here's a friend for you, Billy Bones."

Bones. (*enters UL, dazed with rum*) Who calls? ❷

Jim. Here's a friend for you, Billy Bones. (Pew *pushes* Jim *aside.*)

Bones. Be it—aye, it is Blind Pew! (*reaches for his cutlass*)

Pew. Put your hand down, Bill. (*raises his cane*) I cannot see you, but I can hear a finger stirring. You know why I'm here. Boy,

> ❷ **Predicting**
> What do you think will happen to Billy Bones?

take his hand and bring it near me. Quick! His hand! (Jim *does as he was ordered.* Pew *dramatically puts a piece of paper into the palm of* Bones.) There. It's done. You've been warned, Billy Bones. You've been warned. *(laughs)* Boy, the door? Which way be the door! (Jim, *frightened, starts* Pew *in the right direction.*) And now—I'm off. (Pew *quickly taps out and exits DR.*)

Jim. Shall I stop him?

Bones. Nay, it's too late. They give me the Black Spot.

Jim. What is—the Black Spot?

Bones. It's a summons. *(reads)* "Six o'clock." They'll come to kill me at six o'clock.

Jim. Who?

Bones. All of Flint's crew. I was Flint's first mate, and I'm the only one that knows—knows where the treasure is buried.

Jim. A buried treasure?

Bones. Aye, chests of gold and silver and jewels. A king's fortune it is! And I have the map that shows where the money's buried.

Jim. A map?

Bones. It's the treasure map they want. It's the map they'll kill for. *(choking)* Rum! Get me some rum! So I can swallow! The map is in the chest. *(starts L)* We must get the chest! Aye! Get the chest. *(talks as he exits L, and continues to speak while he is off stage)* Rum! Fetch me some rum, lad!

Jim. I daren't, sir. You're sick and I promised that I wouldn't.

Bones. *(offstage)* Get the Constable! Call the Squire! Tell 'em all to lay on quick at the

Admiral Benbow! Flint's gang is coming for the map. (*enters, dragging the chest*) Lend me a hand, boy. I'll shake them off.

Jim. How?

Bones. I'll ship to another reef. Aye, I'll give them the slip. (*sits on chest, breathing heavily*) A drink of rum, Jim. I'm begging you. A swallow of rum, boy. Look at me. I'm a poor old hulk on a lee shore. And I warn you, lad, if you don't give me a drink and I die a-choking, my blood will drip on you. (*holds up hand which shakes*) Aye, look! My fingers are a-fighting. I've got the shakes, I have. Look. I can see Old Flint. He's there in the corner. Do you see him?

Jim. No. No one is there.

Bones. Morgan . . . and Dirk . . . and Black Dog. Aye, they're all here. Stop! Hold your pace. Knives . . . swords! Ah, a fight you want, is it? I'll fight you. I'll fight you for the map. There! There! Devil take you all! (*He slashes with cutlass, growing more delirious. Suddenly he drops his cutlass, grabs his heart, gives an animal-like cry, and falls, bent over and clutching the sea chest.*)

Jim. Captain? Captain!

Mrs. Hawkins. (*enters UL*) What is it?

Jim. It's the Captain.

Mrs. Hawkins. Another heart attack! Captain! (*She shakes him, then draws back in fear.*) He doesn't move.

Jim. Is he dead?

Mrs. Hawkins. (*puts hand near to* Bones' *nose*) No breath.

Jim. A blind man came and he gave him the Black Spot.

Mrs. Hawkins. He's dead. We must go for help. But, first, I'll claim the money he owes me. (*starts to touch the dead body, but pulls back*) You . . . You, Jim, look in his pocket for a key to the chest.

Jim. Me? (*With fear of the dead, he cautiously searches* Bones' *coat pockets, giving articles to* Mrs. Hawkins.) A knife . . . tobacco. That's all.

Mrs. Hawkins. The key. I'll warrant he wears the key around his neck. Open his collar.

Jim. (*rolls* Bones *forward, off the chest, face up*) It's here. On a string.

Mrs. Hawkins. Use the knife. (Jim *cuts string.*) Give me the key. Yes, it fits. (*She opens chest, lifting items.*) Some papers tied in oilcloth. Ah! Here it is, a bag of money! Now as my witness, Jim, I'll only take what's rightfully mine, and not a farthing over. (*A loud signal whistle is heard, offstage.*)

Jim. Listen. (*A second whistle is heard.*)

Mrs. Hawkins. Someone's whistling.

Jim. It's a signal. They're coming. Quick!

Mrs. Hawkins. First I'll have the money he owes me.

Jim. (*Third whistle is heard.*) It's the pirates for sure!

Mrs. Hawkins. Pirates!

Jim. They're coming closer. Take the bag of money.

Mrs. Hawkins. Yes!

Jim. (*hurries her out*) Quick! Go out the back way!

Mrs. Hawkins. Yes. Come, Jim. Hurry!

Jim. And for the fourpenny you still owe me, I'll take this. (*holds up oilcloth packet*) ❸ Goodby, Billy Bones. (*He hears Pew, looks toward front, then starts UR, stops when he realizes he is trapped.*)

Pew. (*offstage*) Stand guard! Surround the house, mateys. Watch the back door. Shoot if

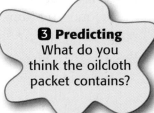

❸ **Predicting**
What do you think the oilcloth packet contains?

a body moves! (*He enters DR. Black Dog* is guiding him. *Dirk follows.*) Where be the door? The door?

Jim. (*desperate, points to closet door*) I'll hide—in the closet! (*He hides, as* Pew *and pirates enter "house."*)

Dirk. (*discovering* Bones *on the floor*) What's here? Look!

Pew. What is it?

Dirk. It's Bill. Billy Bones.

Pew. Where? (*raises his cane to strike*)

Dirk. He's dead.

Pew. Dead?

Dirk. Laying on the floor.

Pew. (*feeling the body*) Are you sure?

Black Dog. Aye, dead he is.

Pew. Search him! Find the map. Look in his pockets.

Dirk. Bill's been overhauled.

Pew. Find the key. The key for the chest.

Black Dog. The chest is here.

Pew. Where? (*feels it with his cane*)

Dirk. Aye, the chest is open.

Pew. The map? The treasure map! Is it there?

Black Dog. Nowhere.

Pew. Find it!

Black Dog. It ain't here. The map's been lifted.

Pew. It's that boy. He's still in the house. I can smell his kitchen apron. Find him!

Dirk. The closet.

Black Dog. Aye, the closet. (*He and* Dirk *go to closet and start to open the door.*)

Pew. Wait. First, take up old Bill. (*Black Dog* and Dirk *pick up* Bones.) Put him in his room. Sit him up nice-like in a chair. Show him some respect. He was Flint's first mate. (*They carry*

Bones *off UL.*) Hoist him aloft. Or we'll be cursed forever by Flint's dead eye. Where are you, boy? I'll find you, boy. *(Jim peeks out, sees that only* Pew *is there, tip-toes out, as* Pew, *tapping with his cane, searches.)* I hear you. I HEAR you. *(Jim freezes.)* I cannot see you, but I know you're here. *(Pew raises his pistol, advancing toward* Jim. Jim *holds up knife, tosses it across DR.* Pew, *alerted by the sound, goes DR, aiming his pistol.)* Ah, there you are! *(laughs)* You thought you could trick me. But you won't get away from Blind Pew. *(calls)* Ahoy, mates! I've got him cornered.

Dirk. *(offstage)* We be coming.

Black Dog. *(offstage)* Aye, we're with you.

Jim. *(caught, with no exit, looks up at fireplace)* No! You haven't got me yet. *(He disappears in the fireplace as* Dirk *and* Black Dog *enter UL.)*

Pew. His voice!

Dirk. Where is he?

Black Dog. No one here.

Pew. I heard him. He talked! Use your eyes! He didn't go up in a puff of smoke. Smoke! *(laughs)* The fireplace. Where be the fireplace?

Black Dog. *(guides him)* Here.

Pew. We've got you now, boy. *(Three whistles are heard off.)*

Dirk. Three whistles! Morgan's giving us the last warning!

Black Dog. Someone's coming.

Dirk. Make for the ship.

Black Dog. Aye, we'll have to budge, mates. (*He and* Dirk *exit DL.*)

Pew. Fools! Wait. You're leaving a fortune behind. We'll be rich as kings when we find the treasure. (*silence*) Black Dog . . . ? Dirk . . . ? Where are you? You ain't leaving me behind? Where are you, mateys? (*desperate to find the way out*) Help me. Which is the way out? Which way? Which way? (*He falls over the chest, accidentally firing the gun. He grabs his chest as he falls, gasping for breath.*) **4**

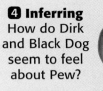

4 Inferring
How do Dirk and Black Dog seem to feel about Pew?

Dogger. (*runs DL*) I heard a gun shot inside the house, sir. (*goes in "house" cautiously*)

Squire. (*He and* Doctor *enter DL.*) Take care. There's trouble all right. It's good I came with you, Doctor.

Doctor. Yes, I'm glad you came, Squire. Is there anyone in the house?

Dogger. Nay, quiet as a tomb.

Doctor. (*He and* Squire *enter "house."*) Yes, they're gone.

Squire. The <u>rogues</u>. They've escaped before we could have the law on them. (*sees* Pew) What's this? Who is he?

Dogger. One of the ruffians. Been shot in the chest, he has.

Doctor. Yes, it looks as if he tripped and shot himself. Come, give him a hand, Dogger. Take him into the back room.

Dogger. (*Helps* Pew, *and they exit UL.*) Yes, sir. Up, man.

Doctor. I'll see what I can do to save his worthless life. (*exits after them*)

Vo•cab•u•lary

rogues (rohgz) people who are unscrupulous or dishonest

Squire. The woman said they were a band of pirates. Gave the Captain the Black Spot.

Jim. (*offstage*) Hel-loooo.

Squire. (*draws pistol*) Who's that?

Jim. (*offstage*) Hel-loooo.

Squire. Who's there?

Jim. (*offstage*) Me.

Squire. Who? Where?

Jim. (*offstage*) In the fireplace.

Squire. (*covers fireplace with pistol*) I have a gun.

Jim. (*offstage*) Don't shoot.

Squire. Come down.

Jim. (*His legs appear in fireplace. offstage*) I can't. My pants are caught on a peg. O-o-o-o-oh! (*He drops to floor, crawls out.*)

Squire. Up with your hands.

Jim. Yes, sir.

Squire. Why, you're the serving boy.

Jim. Yes, sir.

Squire. Stand up.

Jim. (*stands, putting hands behind to cover pants*) My pants are ripped.

Squire. Lucky they didn't rip your belly. Pirates were they?

Jim. (*nods*) They were going to shoot me.

Doctor. (*enters UL*) Who was going to shoot you?

Jim. Blind Pew.

Doctor. And instead he shot himself.

Dogger. (*enters L*) Aye, dead he is.

Doctor. Pick up the pistol, Dogger, and take the chest away. Now, lad, tell the Squire and me what happened. Are you hurt?

Jim. No, sir.

Doctor. Then why are you standing in a twist?

Jim. My trousers are ripped—behind.

Doctor. Never mind that. Speak up.

Jim. They were Flint's men.

Squire. Flint's men?

Jim. They came to get the Captain's sea chest.

Squire. Money?

Jim. No, sir. Not money, I think. But—this. *(holds up oilcloth packet)* I give it to you, Doctor, for safe keeping.

Squire. What is it?

Doctor. *(puts packet away, and pointedly ignores Squire)* Now, Dogger, if you will oblige us by putting the chest back in his room, and take the pistol to the Constable. Tell him the rogues are gone, and that Squire Trelawney and I will give him a full report later.

Dogger. Yes, Doctor. I'll hurry, out the back way. Good day, gentlemen. *(exits UL)*

Squire. Good day.

Doctor. And now, Squire, what was your question? **5**

Squire. The packet! What is in it?

Doctor. *(toying with packet)* Suppose it is a clue to where Flint buried his treasure?

Squire. A map?

Doctor. And if it is a map?

Squire. I will fit out a ship and we will sail and find the treasure.

Doctor. You have made a bargain, Squire. Now, Jim, with your permission, we will open the packet. I need a knife.

Jim. *(picks up knife from floor)* Here. It was the Captain's.

Doctor. We will open his secret with his own knife.

5 Inferring
Why did the doctor ignore the Squire's question at first?

Squire. Hurry, man! Hurry! Is it? Is it? It is!

Doctor. A map!

Squire. Of an island.

Doctor. Latitudes and longitudes.

Squire. And three crosses, marked in red. What does the print say in the corner?

Doctor. "Bulk of treasure buried here."

Squire. It's Flint's treasure map. Doctor, I will keep my bargain. In two weeks we will have the best ship in England. Jim, you will be the cabin-boy. You will be the ship's Doctor. And I will be—Admiral! Ah, I feel like a boy again. Some wine, Jim. We'll drink a toast to our new adventure.

Jim. Yes, sir. (*He crosses, back to audience; remembers his ripped trousers and stops. A piece of bright underwear is seen. He tries to cover it with his hands.*) Yes, sir. (*exits UL*)

Doctor. Squire. There is one danger. There is one man I am afraid of.

Squire. Who is he? Name the dog, sir.

Doctor. You. With your boundless enthusiasm I fear you cannot hold your tongue. This must be a SECRET voyage.

Squire. You are right. My lips are sealed. I will be as silent—
as a grave. (*Jim enters UL with tray and three
mugs.*) Come, Jim. Join us and lift a
cup. (*holds mug out*) A toast to
our new adventure.

Doctor. (*holds out mug*)
A toast to our secret
voyage.

Jim. (*holds mug out*)
A toast to—Treasure
Island!

(*Doctor and Squire turn
to him and "Sh." The
three tip their mugs and
drink, as the Toy Theatre
curtain drops. Music begins,
"The Sailor-oh."*) ○

Answering the BIG Question

As you do the following activities, consider the Big Question:
Which is more important—the journey or the destination?

WRITE TO LEARN Think about the four pirates: Billy Bones, Blind Pew, Dirk, and Black Dog. They've shared journeys, but do they share a bond of loyalty and friendship? Answer this question in your Learner's Notebook.

LITERATURE GROUPS Join with two or three other students who have read "Treasure Island." Discuss the risks and dangers that the trip to Treasure Island will involve. Then, discuss whether the destination is always worth the cost of the journey.

When is the price too high?

Most things that are worth having come at a price. Sometimes the price is well worth it. Other times the price is too high. As you read the following selections, think about how you would answer the question: **When is the price too high?**

Key Reading Skills

As you read the selections in this unit, apply these reading skills.

- **Previewing** Look over the selection and think about what it will be about. Check out the title, any subheads, and any other features that give a clue about the selection.
- **Understanding Text Structures** Look for clues that tell you how the selection is organized.
- **Identifying Main Idea and Supporting Details** Determine the main point of the reading and of its sections. The details support the main idea and help you understand the author's points.
- **Skimming and Scanning** Skimming is looking over a selection to get a general idea of what it is about. Scanning is a quick look to find specific information.

BRANDED BEAUTY

by Shari Graydon

What are people really looking for when they buy brand-name items?

If some people risk their health through attempts to control their bodies, many others risk their finances through efforts to win at the wardrobe game. ❶ More than anyone else, teenagers suffer from the brand-name beauty disease in which certain clothing manufacturers become essential weapons in the beauty power wars.

❶ **Previewing**
Look at the title, the images, and the first sentence to decide what this selection is about.

Whether it's Parasuco in Montreal, American Eagle in the Midwest, or Tommy Hilfiger in California, often what matters in clothing is not the color or the shape, but the name—and the more visible it is, the better. More so than ever before, brands have become a means of saying: "We're beautiful, rich, and important"—and at the same time implying: "If you're not dressed like us, *you're not!*"

Buying the right brand is like having a membership in the "in" crowd, like silently informing everyone around you that you're <u>savvy</u> enough to know what's hot. The chosen brand <u>embodies</u> the irresistible promise of automatic cool to anyone who has the bucks to buy it.

Vo•cab•u•lary

savvy (SAV vee) smart; knowledgeable
embodies (em BAH deez) makes real; puts into visible form

Branded Beauty

But what about those who don't have the bucks?

The pressure to buy the right brand names is so harsh that many kids whose families can't afford them feel <u>compelled</u> to get part-time jobs just so they can dress well around other kids. They trade time to hang out with their friends for the money necessary to have the right clothes to hang out *in*.

Of course, the real power in this beauty equation is held by the brand makers themselves. They're the ones who get rich as a result. Consider the range in price for a pair of blue jeans. The cost of the denim material, thread, and zipper or buttons is often the same, whether the jeans are made by a high-end fashion designer or the local discount chain. But you can pay less than $35 for a no-name brand, or ten times that price—as much as $350—to advertise the Versace name across your tush. ○

LIFE-THREATENING AFFLUENZA

Sometimes wearing brand-name items just isn't worth it.

"Those shoes are to die for!" "I'd kill for a jacket like that!"

Lots of people casually express <u>sentiments</u> like these all the time. Unfortunately, some have actually acted on them. In April 1989, sixteen-

Vo•cab•u•lary

compelled (kum PELD) forced or exerted pressure
sentiments (SEN tuh munts) expressions of an attitude based on feeling instead of reason

year-old Johnny Bates was shot to death in Houston by another teenager when he failed to turn over his Air Jordan high-tops. His fate was shared by other young men in Baltimore, Atlanta, Philadelphia, and Detroit—all shot, strangled, or knifed for their Avia, Nike, or Fila running shoes during the 1980s, when the branding of high-end sneakers went into overdrive.

This kind of extreme behavior is rare, but some critics of commercial hype say it's not surprising in a world that places such high value on <u>conspicuous consumption</u>.

They've even coined the expression "<u>affluenza</u>," suggesting that the willingness to pay way more for this brand over that one is a disease or an illness, like the flu. ○

Answering the BIG Question

As you do the following activities, consider the Big Question:
When is the price too high?

WRITE TO LEARN Think about what motivates people to buy certain items. Write a brief entry in your Learner's Notebook about what factors you think are most important when choosing what to buy.

LITERATURE GROUPS Meet with two or three others who have read "Life-Threatening Affluenza." Discuss what you think leads to the extreme behavior of killing for brand-name items.

Vo•cab•u•lary

conspicuous (kun SPIK yoo us) obvious; easily seen
consumption (kun SUMP shun) the use of goods and services
affluenza (af loo EN zuh) condition of being preoccupied with buying and owning things; combines the words "affluence" (AF loo uns), meaning wealth, and "influenza" (in floo EN zuh), the full name for the flu

Chuy's Beginnings

by René Saldaña, Jr.

A tough guy finds out what it feels like to get what he really wants.

Mr. Gutierrez told me, "Come with me, Chuy." On the way to the office he was walking fast in front of me, making like I wasn't even there, and I could've just turned down a ramp and took off running to Leo's Grocery, played hooky the rest of the day, played on the Centipede video game. He wouldn't've ever noticed me gone. Like I was invisible.

He just kept walking while I kept asking, "What's the matter, Mr. G?" No answer, so I said, "<u>Vato</u>, you think you're the boss?" **❶**

❶ Skimming
Look over the story to find out what happens to Chuy.

"In *my* classroom, I *am* the boss!" Mr. Gutierrez screamed at me just outside the principal's office. He'd been walking so fast that when he turned around, he caught me off guard and I almost ran into him.

Ah, you ain't nothing, I thought.

A few minutes back, he'd kicked me out of his class for just talking. "Step outside and wait to the right of the door, and don't move from there, Chuy," he'd said.

"<u>Órale</u>," I said.

When he came out, he didn't even explain why he'd yelled at me, just stood there and looked at his watch, his back to me the whole time, until one of the office aides showed up and he said to her, "They know what they're supposed to be doing. I'll try not to take too long."

So now outside the office I told him, "Whatever, Boss." I took hold of the doorknob, swung open the door, and said, "Well, let's do this thing."

"Let's," he said.

Vo·cab·u·lary

vato (VAH toh) buddy, pal (informal Mexican Spanish)
órale (OH rah lay) come on (informal Mexican Spanish)

Sure enough, when we got in to see Mrs. Mendez, Gutierrez told her his side of the story: "I've warned Chuy several times already," he began. "And I've got the paperwork to prove it."

Mrs. Mendez listened, her scalp showing through her thinning hair, shining in the light coming through the window behind her. When she raised a finger to speak, he kept on going, he waved her off: "And believe you me, Mrs. Mendez, I've put enough energy into this Time Out strategy this school district has adopted, especially with Chuy, too much energy and time, time I could be spending with the students who are in class to learn."

"Name one who really wants to learn," I said.

He looked at me, then back at Mrs. Mendez, and went on: "It's been time wasted, all those chances, to no avail. I'm done using that approach with Chuy. It hasn't worked. So I want something done about this. And until something is done, I won't accept him back into my classroom."

Mrs. Mendez cleared her gargly throat and swallowed the gargajo. She looked at me and said, "And what's your side?"

I said, "Nothing." I knew their game. I'd say something, anything, right or wrong, and somehow I'd end up in more trouble than I was in already. Two weeks of in-school suspension versus two months. It was all

Vo•cab•u•lary

gargajo (gar AH hoh) mucus (informal Spanish)

the same to me. It was easy there; the coaches saw to it we were quiet and the cafeteria people brought us our trays of food. And like Mrs. Mendez really cared anyway. She was one of them, *the* one of them. They had each other's backs.

"You're not here in my office for 'nothing,'" she said. "If you don't speak up now, then I'll have to take Mr. Gutierrez's account as the final word. You could help yourself."

Or hurt myself, I thought. There it was—part of their plan—doomed if I did, doomed if I didn't. I decided to keep my mouth shut.

Except for Mr. G had to go and mess it up for me: "You're all about talking in the classroom, que eres un gangster pa'ca and that you're the tough guy pa'lla, and that ni Mrs. Mendez nor the cops can touch you[1], all big and tough in the class," he said. "Why won't you say anything now?—to her face, vato."

I freaked out. I'd never heard Mr. G talk like this; he'd always gone on proper and right and boring. This was something else.

"So?" asked Mrs. Mendez.

"Nothing at all," I said. "I don't know what bug crawled up Mr. G's butt and died."

"Excuse me?" she said.

Mr. G slapped at the armrest. "You see what I've got to put up with? I won't have any more of this."

And all of a sudden it was back to his old college-word-using self: "I expect you to act accordingly," he told Mrs. Mendez.

"I certainly will," she said. "Mr. Gutierrez, if you would step outside and fill out a referral. And get

....

[1] Mr. Guttierez is mixing Mexican slang with English. The sentence means: "You're always talking in the classroom about how you're a gangster over here and a tough guy over there, and that neither Mrs. Mendez nor the cops can touch you..."

me copies of all the paperwork you've got on Chuy."

"Gladly, ma'am," he said, and left.

He shut the door behind him, and Mrs. Mendez was clicking away at her computer. I sat back to try to think things through. She wanted paperwork on me and she'd get plenty of it. If Mr. G was good at one thing, it was at keeping paperwork. He'd stop class in the middle of a lesson on the comma, or reading aloud; one time he stopped reading out of *Rumble Fish* just to write down that one of his students was misbehaving, and all the students booed him. He took his sweet time doing it, and since there was only one copy of the book, we had to wait for him to finish to get back to reading.

He'd stopped lessons because of me more times than I could count. I'd seen his journal once, the one he kept just for school things, and it was halfway filled with his notes: a date at the top, the time, a short title like "Chuy talking out of turn," and then a note. He always put the journal in his backpack when he was done.

"Chuy," said Mrs. Mendez, "why do you keep doing this? Getting in trouble, I mean? One of these days, you're going to cry wolf and no one's going to pay any attention to you."

"What?" I asked.

"If I know Mr. Gutierrez at all, I'm sure he's got plenty of notes on you, and I can't do anything to help you out if he's got everything documented. I see in my records," she said, and pointed at the computer screen in front of her, "that we've sent you to in-school suspension plenty already. Your days in there have run out. The next step, according to the rules, is a trip to the alternative center." **2**

2 Identifying Main Idea
What is the main idea of this paragraph?

"What?" I said. "For talking when G's going on about something boring!"

"It's the next step," she said. "Rules are rules. You give us no way out. You've used up all the chances we can give."

"Listen, Miss," I said, and turned on the charm, "I swear, give me one more chance—ISS or after-school suspension, whatever— but one more chance, and I'll show you I can behave. I don't even have to be put into Mr. G's class. Send me to another teacher; Mr. Herrera, he's cool."

She looked like she was considering my idea, then said, "Chuy, I'll tell you what, let me think about this. Take a seat out there. In a few minutes I'll come out and tell you my decision."

"Thanks so much, Miss. You won't regret it."

I was talking to the secretary when Mr. G came in with his journal and started making copies, one page after another.

Mrs. Mendez called him into her office. "I'll talk to you in a bit, Chuy." She smiled a little, so I knew I'd talked her into letting me stay here and not sending me to the alternative center. Only losers ended up there. I was no loser.

In a few moments, I heard the door open, Mr. G came out, shaking his head, and said, "I guess you won't need these copies, if that's your decision. Some system we've got going here. Perpetuating bad behavior. Wonderful!" he said. "It's a surprise so many of us stay at this job as long as we do." Then to me: "You are one lucky sonofagun. But you won't ever amount to much if you keep up this behavior. Good luck."

"Yeah, whatever, dude."

So she called me in next. "You won't be going to the alternative center. I'm counting on you, Chuy."

I nodded.

"Here's what's going to happen."

I listened, and inside I was all relieved. I'd have to help clean up the cafeteria after lunch, and I was going to be put in Mr. Herrera's class. My friends had told me he was easy, played the radio and let his students talk all the time.

"But this is your last chance," she said. "Appreciate what you're being given here."

"I do," I told her. Maybe I was wrong about her.

"Just wait outside for a few more minutes. I have to work out your schedule, okay?"

"Okay," I said, and sat down outside again.

I had started talking to the secretary when Mr. G came in huffing. He didn't even knock on Mrs. Mendez's door, just burst in on her and slammed it shut. I heard them shouting and all of us got quiet, me, the secretary, and the couple kids who had come in to hand in the attendance sheets. Something about "If this is how this district treats its teachers," then I don't know what else because Mrs. Mendez starting yelling about how she was "the final word in this school" and she was "looking out for the welfare of her charges," and he said, "Speaking of charges, if nothing real is done to remedy this situation, I'll be calling my union rep and filing charges of my own."

Then Mr. G yanked the door open, walked out, I stood up, and he glared at me: "Happy?" he said.

"Siroles," I said. "I couldn't be happier."

But really, I felt bad because he was an okay guy and he had given me one chance after another, like the time when I pushed Lee up against the wall for hiding my notebook and Mr. G came to Lee's defense. He said, "Earlier in the day, if you remember right, Chuy, you took Lee's notebook and just tore a couple of sheets of his paper without asking. If you want him to respect your possessions, you have to respect his."

I screamed, "Tú me vales!" and all he did was look sad.

Instead of calling security for me cursing him in front of the whole class or writing me a referral, he sat down at his desk, all calm, then got up and went back to helping the other students with their work. Everyone was real quiet the rest of the hour, and nobody looked at me. G didn't even write me up in his journal.

Vo•cab•u•lary

siroles (see ROH les) sure (informal Mexican Spanish)
tú me vales (too meh VAH les) you're worthless (informal Mexican Spanish)

The next day I apologized to him, private, before class got started. Mrs. Mendez didn't have that one on her computer. **3**

Today I also felt bad because the only other people I ever heard fighting were my parents, and then I just locked myself up in my room. Today G had screamed at Mrs. Mendez and she yelled at him. They both looked angry. I felt like crying, truth be told.

I called after Mr. G. He turned and said, "What do you want, Chuy? You want to spit in my face next?"

3 Scanning
Look for key words that tell you how Chuy really feels about what has happened with Mr. Gutierrez.

I said, "Ah, man, no way. I want to say I'm sorry. If you want, I can explain it to Mrs. Mendez."

"Explain what?" Mr. G asked, full up on me now. "That you don't care one iota for anyone but yourself? I thought you'd be happy now—I'll probably get fired for my little stunt, but you know what, I'll take full responsibility for my actions, unlike you."

"Man," I said, "I just want to try to fix this."

"How? Give her that famous smile of yours and then everything will be okay like it always is?" He walked out the door, and the door eased shut, slow, letting the heat from outside hit me in the face.

I heard Mrs. Mendez inside her office behind her door typing away, but real fast, like she didn't have enough time to type it all but she had to try.

I stood there in the leftover heat, my face just beginning to feel the cool of the air-conditioning. The door clicked shut, the secretary took a phone call, hung up, then knocked on Mrs. Mendez's door. She closed it behind her and I could hear one of them, maybe both of them, crying little baby cries. I imagined them holding each other, and I wished—never mind what I wished. Today I'd made Mrs. Mendez cry, and I'd probably gotten Mr. G fired—I was something else. ○

Answering the BIG Question

As you do the following activities, consider the Big Question:
When is the price too high?

WRITE TO LEARN Think about the last line of the story, "I was something else." In your Learner's Notebook, write what you think Chuy means by this.

PARTNER TALK Join with a partner who has read this story. Talk about how this story relates to the Big Question. What price does Chuy pay for his behavior in Mr. Gutierrez's class? Who else in the story pays a price for the choices they have made?

I Escaped the Taliban

by Kristin Baird Rattini

What would make a girl give up everything for the unknown?

When Nargis Alizadeh remembers her childhood in
Afghanistan, she remembers fear. Life was dangerous for her
family under the Taliban government. They banned TV, radio,
and photographs. Women weren't allowed to attend school or
even go outside without a man. Those who didn't obey were
jailed—or killed. "They took away our happiness," Nargis says.
"They put fear in people's hearts so they wouldn't disobey the
rules."

After the Taliban found out that Nargis's father had been
teaching women, the family knew he had to escape Afghanistan
immediately. A year and a half later, Nargis, her younger sister
and brother, and their mother also made the break for the border
between Afghanistan and Iran—and for freedom. "I was really

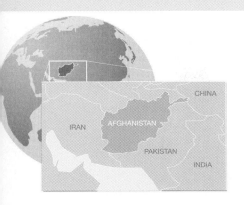

scared," Nargis says. "If we were caught, we would be killed."

They left in darkness, carrying only two blankets and a few clothes. Anything else might attract thieves. The next night, they struggled through the rain on a three-hour journey across muddy trails. "Those three hours felt as long as three days," she says.

"Our feet were numb because it was so cold." **1**

They walked in silence—and fear. At any moment the family could face wolves, wild dogs, or worse: soldiers who would arrest them. After crossing a swift, swollen river and paying guards $5,000 to let them into Iran, Nargis and her family finally made it across the border.

1 Understanding Text Structures In what order does the article tell Nargis's story?

Reunited with her father, Nargis and her family now live in San Diego, California. And she's grateful for the journey she made eight years ago. "I appreciate everything I have in the United States," says Nargis. "I have the freedom to go to school, practice my religion, and make my dreams come true." ○

Answering the BIG Question

As you do the following activities, consider the Big Question:
When is the price too high?

WRITE TO LEARN Think about life under the Taliban as described in this article. Write a brief entry in your Learner's Notebook about what you think it was like to live under such harsh rules.

LITERATURE GROUPS Meet with two or three other students who have read "I Escaped the Taliban." Discuss what hardships would make a person leave his or her home and/or country.

The RAVINE

by Graham Salisbury

A boy must decide what it's worth to him to prove to his friends that he's not a wimp.

When Vinny and three others dropped down into the ravine, they entered a jungle thick with tangled trees and rumors of what might have happened to the dead boy's body. ❶

The muddy trail was slick and, in places where it had fallen away, flat-out dangerous. The cool breeze that swept the Hawaiian hillside pastures above died early in the descent.

There were four of them—Vinny; his best friend, Joe-Boy; Mo, who was afraid of nothing; and Joe-Boy's *haole* girlfriend, Starlene—all fifteen. It was a Tuesday in July, two weeks and a day after the boy had drowned. If, in fact, that's what had happened to him.

Vinny slipped, and dropped his towel in the mud. He picked it up and tried to brush it off, but instead smeared the mud spot around until the towel resembled something someone's dog had slept on. "Tst," he said.

Joe-Boy, hiking down just behind him, laughed. "Hey, Vinny, just think, that kid walked where you walking."

"Shuddup," Vinny said.

"You prob'ly stepping right where his foot was."

Vinny moved to the edge of the trail, where the ravine fell through a twisted jungle of gnarly trees and underbrush to the stream far below.

❶ **Skimming and Scanning**
Skim the story to discover why the ravine is a challenge to the characters. Then scan to see how many characters meet the challenge.

Vo•cab•u•lary

ravine (ruh VEEN) a deep, narrow valley
descent (dee SENT) a move down from a higher place
haole (HOW lee) a Hawaiian term for a white person
gnarly (NAR lee) twisted and lumpy

Joe-Boy laughed again. "You such a queen, Vinny. You know that?"

Vinny could see Starlene and Mo farther ahead, their heads bobbing as they walked, both almost down to the pond where the boy had died.

"Hey," Joe-Boy went on, "maybe you going be the one to find his body."

"You don't cut it out, Joe-Boy, I going . . . I going . . ."

"What, cry?"

Vinny scowled. Sometimes Joe-Boy was a big fat babooze.

They slid down the trail. Mud oozed between Vinny's toes. He grabbed at roots and branches to keep from falling. Mo and Starlene were out of sight now, the trail ahead having cut back.

Joe-Boy said, "You going jump in the water and go down and your hand going touch his face, stuck under the rocks. *Ha ha ha . . . a ha ha ha!*"

Vinny <u>winced</u>. He didn't want to be here. It was too soon, way too soon. Two weeks and one day.

He saw a footprint in the mud and stepped around it.

The dead boy had jumped and had never come back up. Four search and rescue divers hunted for two days straight and never found him. Not a trace. Gave Vinny the creeps. It didn't make sense. The pond wasn't that big.

He wondered why it didn't seem to bother anyone else. Maybe it did and they just didn't want to say.

Butchie was the kid's name. Only fourteen.

Fourteen.

Two weeks and one day ago he was walking down this trail. Now nobody could find him.

Vo·cab·u·lary

winced (winst) flinched

The jungle crushed in, reaching over the trail, and Vinny brushed leafy branches aside. The roar of the waterfall got louder, louder.

Starlene said it was the goddess that took him, the one that lives in the stone down by the road. She did that every now and then, Starlene said, took somebody when she got lonely. Took him and kept him. Vinny had heard that legend before, but he'd never believed in it.

Now he didn't know what he believed.

The body had to be stuck down there. But still, four divers and they couldn't find it?

Vinny decided he'd better believe in the legend. If he didn't, the goddess might get mad and send him bad luck. Or maybe take *him*, too.

Stopstopstop! Don't think like that.

"Come on," Joe-Boy said, nudging Vinny from behind. "Hurry it up."

Just then Starlene whooped, her voice bouncing around the walls of the ravine.

"Let's *go*," Joe-Boy said. "They there already."

Moments later, Vinny jumped up onto a large boulder at the edge of the pond. Starlene was swimming out in the brown water. It wasn't murky brown, but clean and clear to a depth of maybe three or four feet. Because of the waterfall you had to yell if you wanted to say something. The whole place smelled of mud and ginger and iron.

Starlene swam across to the waterfall on the far side of the pond and ducked under it, then climbed out and edged along the rock wall behind it, moving slowly, like a spider. Above, sun-sparkling stream water spilled over the lip of a one-hundred-foot drop.

Mo and Joe-Boy threw their towels onto the rocks and dove into the pond. Vinny watched, his muddy towel hooked around his neck. Reluctantly, he let it fall, then dove in after them.

The cold mountain water tasted <u>tangy</u>. Was it because the boy's body was down there <u>decomposing</u>? He spit it out.

He followed Joe-Boy and Mo to the waterfall and ducked under it. They climbed up onto the rock ledge, just as Starlene had done, then spidered their way over to where you could climb to a small ledge about fifteen feet up. They took their time because the hand and footholds were slimy with moss.

Starlene jumped first. Her shriek echoed off the rocky cliff, then died in the dense green jungle.

Mo jumped, then Joe-Boy, then Vinny.

The fifteen-foot ledge was not the problem.

It was the one above it, the one you had to work up to, the big one, where you had to take a deadly zigzag trail that climbed up and away from the waterfall, then cut back and forth to a foot-wide ledge something more like fifty feet up.

That was the problem.

That was where the boy had jumped from.

Joe-Boy and Starlene swam out to the middle of the pond. Mo swam back under the waterfall and climbed once again to the fifteen-foot ledge.

Vinny started to swim out toward Joe-Boy but stopped when he saw Starlene put her arms around him. She kissed him. They sank under for a long time, then came back up, still kissing.

Joe-Boy saw Vinny looking and winked. "You like that, Vinny? Watch, I show you how." He kissed Starlene again.

Vo·cab·u·lary

tangy (TANG ee) sharp and strong in smell or taste
decomposing (dee kum POH zing) decaying; rotting

Vinny turned away and swam back over to the other side of the pond, where he'd first gotten in. His mother would kill him if she ever heard about where he'd come. After the boy drowned, or was taken by the goddess, or whatever happened to him, she said never to come to this pond again. Ever. It was off-limits. Permanently.

But not his dad. He said, "You fall off a horse, you get back on, right? Or else you going be scared of it all your life."

His mother scoffed and waved him off. "Don't listen to him, Vinny, listen to me. Don't go there. That pond is haunted." Which had made his dad laugh.

But Vinny promised he'd stay away.

But then Starlene and Joe-Boy said, "Come with us anyway. You let your mommy run your life, or what?" And Vinny said, "But what if I get caught?" And Joe-Boy said, "So?"

Vinny mashed his lips. He was so weak. Couldn't even say no. But if he'd said, "I can't go, my mother won't like it," they would have laughed him right off the island. No, he had to go. No choice. ❷

So he'd come along, and so far it was fine. He'd even gone in the water. Everyone was happy. All he had to do now was wait it out and go home and hope his mother never heard about it.

When he looked up, Starlene was gone.

He glanced around the pond until he spotted her starting up the zigzag trail to the fifty-foot ledge. She was moving slowly,

> ❷ **Understanding Text Structures**
> The author is using a problem-solution text structure. What problem does the main character face?

Vo•cab•u•lary

scoffed (skawft) was scornful or mocking

hanging on to roots and branches on the upside of the cliff. He couldn't believe she was going there. He wanted to yell, *Hey, Starlene, that's where he died!*

But she already knew that.

Mo jumped from the lower ledge, yelling, "Banzaiiii!" An explosion of coffee-colored water erupted when he hit.

Joe-Boy swam over to where Starlene had gotten out. He waved to Vinny, grinning like a fool, then followed Starlene up the zigzag trail.

Now Starlene was twenty-five, thirty feet up. Vinny watched her for a while, then lost sight of her when she slipped behind a wall of jungle that blocked his view. A few minutes later she popped back out, now almost at the top, where the trail ended, where there was nothing but mud and a few plants to grab on to if you slipped, plants that would rip right out of the ground, plants that wouldn't stop you if you fell, nothing but your screams between you and the rocks below.

Vinny's stomach tingled just watching her. He couldn't imagine what it must feel like to be up there, especially if you were afraid of heights, like he was. *She has no fear*, Vinny thought, *no fear at all. Pleasepleaseplease, Starlene. I don't want to see you die.*

Starlene crept forward, making her way to the end of the trail, where the small ledge was.

Joe-Boy popped out of the jungle behind her. He stopped, waiting for her to jump before going on.

Vinny held his breath.

Starlene, in her cutoff jeans and soaked T-shirt, stood perfectly still, her arms at her sides. Vinny suddenly felt like hugging her. Why, he couldn't tell. *Starlene, please.*

She reached behind her and took a wide leaf from a plant, then eased down and scooped up a finger of mud. She made a brown cross on her forehead, then wiped her muddy fingers on her jeans.

She waited.

Was she thinking about the dead boy?

She stuck the stem end of the leaf in her mouth, leaving the rest of it to hang out. When she jumped, the leaf would flap up and cover her nose and keep water from rushing into it. An old island trick.

She jumped.

Down, down.

Almost in slow motion, it seemed at first, then faster and faster. She fell feet first, arms flapping to keep balance so she wouldn't land on her back, or stomach, which would probably almost kill her.

Just before she hit, she crossed her arms over her chest and vanished within a small explosion of rusty water.

Vinny stood, not breathing at all, praying.

Ten seconds. Twenty, thirty . . .

She came back up, laughing.

She shouldn't make fun that way, Vinny thought. It was dangerous, disrespectful. It was asking for it.

Vinny looked up when he heard Joe-Boy shout, "Hey, Vinny, watch how a man does it! Look!"

Joe-Boy scooped up some mud and drew a stroke of lightning across his chest. When he jumped, he threw himself out, face and body parallel to the pond, his arms and legs spread out. *He's crazy*, Vinny thought, *absolutely insane*. At the last second Joe-Boy folded into a ball and hit. *Ca-roomp!* He came up whooping and yelling, *"Wooo! So good!* Come on, Vinny, it's hot!"

Vinny faked a laugh. He waved, shouting, "Naah, the water's too cold!"

Now Mo was heading up the zigzag trail—Mo, who hardly ever said a word and would do anything anyone ever challenged him to do. *Come on, Mo, not you, too.*

Vinny knew then that he would have to jump.

Jump, or never live it down.

Mo jumped in the same way Joe-Boy had, man-style, <u>splayed</u> out in a suicide fall. He came up grinning.

Starlene and Joe-Boy turned toward Vinny.

Vinny got up and hiked around the edge of the pond, walking in the muddy shallows, looking at a school of small brown-backed fish near a ginger patch.

Maybe they'd forget about him.

Starlene <u>torpedoed</u> over, swimming underwater. Her body glittered in the small amount of sunlight that penetrated the trees around the rim of the ravine. When she came up, she broke the surface smoothly, gracefully, like a swan. Her blond hair sleeked back like river grass.

She smiled a sweet smile. "Joe-Boy says you're afraid to jump. I didn't believe him. He's wrong, right?"

Vinny said quickly, "Of course he's wrong. I just don't want to, that's all. The water's cold."

"Naah, it's nice."

Vinny looked away. On the other side of the pond Joe-Boy and Mo were on the cliff behind the waterfall.

"Joe-Boy says your mom told you not to come here. Is that true?"

Vinny nodded. "Yeah. Stupid, but she thinks it's haunted."

"She's right."

"What?"

Vo•cab•u•lary

splayed (splayd) turned outward in an awkward manner
torpedoed (tor PEE dohd) attacked, struck, or moved like a torpedo

"That boy didn't die, Vinny. The stone goddess took him. He's in a good place right now. He's her prince."

Vinny scowled. He couldn't tell if Starlene was teasing him or if she really believed that. He said, "Yeah, prob'ly."

"Are you going to jump, or is Joe-Boy right?"

"Joe-Boy's an idiot. Sure I'm going to jump."

Starlene grinned, staring at Vinny a little too long. "He is an idiot, isn't he? But I love him."

"Yeah, well . . ."

"Go to it, big boy. I'll be watching."

Starlene sank down and swam out into the pond.

Ca-ripes.

Vinny ripped a <u>hank</u> of white ginger from the ginger patch and smelled it, and prayed he'd still be alive after the sun went down.

He took his time climbing the zigzag trail. When he got to the part where the jungle hid him from view, he stopped and smelled the ginger again. So sweet and alive it made Vinny wish for all he was worth that he was climbing out of the ravine right now, heading home.

But of course, there was no way he could do that.

Not before jumping.

He tossed the ginger onto the muddy trail and continued on. He slipped once or twice, maybe three times. He didn't keep track. He was too numb now, too caught up in the insane thing he was about to do. He'd never been this far up the trail before. Once he'd tried to go all the way, but couldn't. It made him dizzy.

Vo•cab•u•lary

hank (hank) a looped or coiled bundle

When he stepped out and the jungle opened into a huge bowl where he could look down, way, way down, he could see their three heads in the water, heads with arms moving slowly to keep them afloat, and a few bright rays of sunlight pouring down onto them, and when he saw this, his stomach fluttered and rose. Something sour came up and he spit it out.

It made him wobble to look down. He closed his eyes. His whole body trembled. The trail was no wider than the length of his foot. And it was wet and muddy from little <u>rivulets</u> of water that bled from the side of the cliff.

The next few steps were the hardest he'd ever taken in his life. He tried not to look down, but he couldn't help it. His gaze was drawn there. He struggled to push back an urge to fly, just jump off and fly. He could almost see himself spiraling down like a glider, or a bird, or a leaf.

His hands shook as if he were freezing. He wondered, *Had the dead boy felt this way? Or had he felt brave, like Starlene or Joe-Boy, or Mo, who seemed to feel nothing.*

Somebody from below shouted, but Vinny couldn't make it out over the waterfall, roaring down just feet beyond the ledge where he would soon be standing, <u>cascading</u> past so close its mist dampened the air he breathed.

The dead boy had just come to the ravine to have fun, Vinny thought. Just a regular kid like himself, come to swim and be with his friends, then go home and eat macaroni and cheese and watch TV, maybe play with his dog or wander around after dark.

But he'd done none of that.

Where was he?

Inch by inch Vinny made it to the ledge. He stood, swaying slightly, the tips of his toes one small movement from the <u>precipice</u>.

Vo•cab•u•lary

rivulets (RIV yoo lets) small streams or ripples
cascading (kas KAYD ing) falling like a waterfall
precipice (PRES uh pis) a steep cliff

Far below, Joe-Boy waved his arm back and forth. It was dreamy to see—back and forth, back and forth. He looked so small down there.

For a moment Vinny's mind went blank, as if he were in some trance, some dream where he could so easily lean out and fall, and think or feel nothing.

A breeze picked up and moved the trees on the ridgeline, but not a breath of it reached the fifty-foot ledge.

Vinny thought he heard a voice, small and distant. Yes. Something inside him, a tiny voice pleading, *Don't do it. Walk away. Just turn and go and walk back down.*

". . . I can't," Vinny whispered.

You can, you can, you can. Walk back down.

Vinny waited.

And waited.

Joe-Boy yelled, then Starlene, both of them waving.

Then something very strange happened.

Vinny felt at peace. Completely and totally calm and at peace. He had not made up his mind about jumping. But something else inside him had.

Thoughts and feelings swarmed, stinging him: *Jump! Jump! Jump! Jump!*

But deep inside, where the peace was, where his mind wasn't, he would not jump. He would walk back down.

No! No, no, no!

Vinny eased down and fingered up some mud and made a cross on his chest, big and bold. He grabbed a leaf, stuck it in his mouth. *Be calm, be calm. Don't look down.*

After a long pause he spit the leaf out and rubbed the cross to a blur.

They walked out of the ravine in silence, Starlene, Joe-Boy, and Mo far ahead of him. They hadn't said a word since he'd come down off the trail. He knew what they were thinking. He knew, he knew, he knew.

At the same time the peace was still there. He had no idea what it was. But he prayed it wouldn't leave him now, prayed it wouldn't go away, would never go away, because in there, in that place where the peace was, it didn't matter what they thought.

Vinny emerged from the ravine into a brilliance that surprised him. Joe-Boy, Starlene, and Mo were now almost down to the road.

Vinny breathed deeply, and looked up and out over the island. He saw, from there, a land that rolled away like honey, easing down a descent of rich Kikuyu grass pastureland, flowing from there over vast highlands of brown and green, then, finally, falling massively to the coast and flat blue sea.

He'd never seen anything like it.

Had it always been here? This view of the island?

He stared and stared, then sat, taking it in.

He'd never seen anything so beautiful in all his life. ○

Answering the BIG Question

As you do the following activities, consider the Big Question:
When is the price too high?

WRITE TO LEARN Think about the conflict described in this story. Then write a brief entry in your Learner's Notebook about a situation in which the desire to fit in with a group can create pressure or conflict.

LITERATURE GROUPS Meet with two or three others who have read "The Ravine." Discuss why people may have a hard time telling their friends they don't want to do something.

MILITARY TESTS MAY HARM WHALES, STUDY SAYS

by John Roach and Sarah Ives

Scientists puzzle over the mystery of dying whales.

In September 2002, people found dead whales on the beaches of the Canary Islands near Africa. ❶ Four hours earlier, international military tests had sent sound waves underwater nearby. Some scientists believe there is a connection between the tests and the whale deaths.

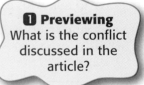

❶ Previewing
What is the conflict discussed in the article?

When scuba divers rise to the ocean surface too quickly, they get the bends, which can be deadly. The bends happen when gas bubbles in blood are released too quickly into surrounding body tissues.

Some scientists believe whales may also get the bends when they rise too fast—and some scientists think that underwater noise from military testing may be causing the whales to rise too fast.

This underwater noise comes from sonar, a technology that sends sound waves into the ocean. Soldiers listen for the sound to bounce off an object. Using sonar, they can tell how far away they are from the object. Militaries use sonar to find submarines and other objects.

The noise seems to harm whales. Research done by the Institute for Animal Health at the University of Las Palmas de Gran Canaria in Spain attempts to show how.

Other scientists agree that sonar hurts whales, but they are not sure that the bends are the cause.

"None of the authors of the research is an expert on [the bends] and none of the results have been seen by anyone who is an expert on [the bends]," said Roger Gentry, a scientist with the U.S. National Marine Fisheries Service. Gentry studies marine mammal strandings.

The Canary Islands deaths were not the first examples of sonar possibly hurting whales. Similar events have happened in Greece and the Bahamas.

Environmentalists, such as Joel Reynolds from the National Resources Defense Council, are trying to stop these deaths. They say that the military needs to work with non-military scientists to make sure that sonar is not harming whales.

A U.S. district court judge in California agreed, ordering the U.S. Navy to talk with environmental groups before doing sonar testing.

Some scientists hope that the court order will help prevent whale deaths. ○

Answering the
BIG Question

As you do the following activities, consider the Big Question:
When is the price too high?

WRITE TO LEARN Think about how sonar testing may hurt whales. Write a brief entry in your Learner's Notebook about whether the benefits of military testing outweigh the danger to whales.

PARTNER TALK Get together with a partner who has read this selection. Discuss ways people are working to reduce the threat to whales from military testing.

RAGNAR'S ROCK

by Douglas Holgate

Is there too high a price to pay for getting everything you've ever dreamed of?

LOKI!? WHAT'S *HE* DOING ON OUR FAMILY MARKER?

163

165

WRITE TO LEARN
Write an entry in your Learner's Notebook about an ambition that's important to you. What would you be willing to give up to achieve this goal? What wouldn't you give up, even if it meant failing?

little MAN

by Hope
Anita Smith

What's it worth to be somebody's hero?

My brother is pounding on the door.
Rap, rap, rap.
"Let. Me. In."
Both sounds working together in
two-part harmony.
I am trying not to hear him.
I lie on my bed
with my fingers laced behind my head
and I smile big.
Because it feels good to be alone.
And even though I can't hear the silence,
when I close my eyes I can almost see it.
But then I hear the volcano
that is my momma's voice
erupt
as she calls my name,

"Cameron James!"
And I know that my <u>solitude</u> is over.
I open the door quickly.
Momma's eyes ask me if I've lost my mind.
My brother's face is tear-stained
and shows he has been betrayed by his hero.
Grandmomma pretends to take no notice
of the situation.
No one says a word.
This is not the silence I had in mind.
So I say,
"Sometimes
a man needs a little privacy!"

Grandmomma clears her throat and says,
"I reckon that's true.
Sometimes a man does need a little privacy."
She can't hold back a laugh when she adds,
"Now, you let your brother back in that room
'cause, I know for a fact,
we could fit the whole
tabernacle choir in there
and you'd still have enough privacy
for the amount of man you are!" ○

Vo·cab·u·lary

solitude (SAWL uh tood) the state of being alone

To MALCOLM X
by Julius Thompson

he knew someone
would take his
life. he lived
never fearing
when the end
would come.
he was a true
brother. he
realized before
the Time
that all men
are men
and children
of each other.
this was his
greatness,
to bring to us
that all men
are really brothers. ○

Answering the BIG Question

As you do the following activities, consider the Big Question:
When is the price too high?

WRITE TO LEARN Think about the attitudes of Malcolm X and Cameron James toward their position as heroes in somebody's life. In your Learner's Notebook, write a brief entry comparing them.

LITERATURE GROUPS Get together with two or three others who have read these poems. Talk about how being looked up to could change a person. How do you think his little brother's feelings shaped Cameron James?

THE RAIDERS JACKET

by Gary Soto

A girl's hopes for romance fall flat when she plays fast with the truth.

Lorena Rocha parted the curtain in her living room and looked out onto the wet street. The rain was still coming down but with less windblown fury. A <u>shaft</u> of sunlight even appeared, poking through the elm tree at the curb. Lorena smiled and then stopped. The sunlight <u>faltered</u> and disappeared as a cloud once again blocked the sun. **1**

Earlier that Saturday morning it had been coming down, as her father said at breakfast, "<u>como gatos y perros</u>." If it didn't stop raining soon it would ruin her day. She

1 Skimming
Who are the main characters in this story, and where does it take place?

Vo•cab•u•lary

shaft (shaft) a straight beam or ray
faltered (FAWL turd) moved in an unsure way; hesitated
como gatos y perros (KO mo GAH tos ee PAIR ros) like cats and dogs (Spanish)

wanted her mother to drive her to the mall at Fashion Fair, but her mother didn't like to drive in rain—and for a good reason: driving in the rain, she had once gotten into an accident that ripped a mailbox from its cemented bolts.

Lorena and her best friend since first grade, Guadalupe, were desperate to go to the mall. They had to replace a Raiders jacket.

The Wednesday before, Eddie Contreras, the handsomest seventh-grader in their class (if not all of Fresno, California), had given Lorena his jacket to wear.

She had been after Eddie <u>relentlessly</u> since September, and in the second week of October, during lunch, he finally took off his jacket and draped it over Lorena's shoulders. She smiled like a queen. She could feel the warmth of his body in the jacket. Her cheeks blossomed into twin roses of happiness.

"OK, but I want it back tomorrow," he said, walking away with his friend Frankie Medina, who looked back, winked, and gave Lorena the thumbs-up sign.

"*Qué guapo*," Guadalupe had said. "I think he likes you."

"Do you think so?" Lorena asked, twirling so that the jacket flared. The sleeves were long and hid her hands. And the collar was as itchy as her father's face at the end of a workday. Still, it was hers for one day. She pushed her hands into the pockets and found a piece of chewing gum, which she tore in half and shared with Guadalupe. It was Juicy Fruit, their favorite.

The two of them were happy and walked around the school yard, parading for all their friends. One girl snapped the gum in her mouth and asked point-blank, "You and Eddie tight?" Lorena didn't answer. Embarrassed, she hid her face behind the sleeves of Eddie's jacket.

When the bell rang Lorena and Guadalupe separated. Lorena went to French class, where she sat warm as a bird in the nest

---

Vo•cab•u•lary

relentlessly (rih LENT liss lee) steadily and without interruption
qué guapo (kay GWAH poh) how handsome (Spanish)

of Eddie's jacket. She went dreamy with deep longing. She kept picturing herself and Eddie running in slow motion down a windswept beach, each of them wearing a Raiders jacket, each of them draped in silver and black. Her smiling face was soft, with a faraway look. When the teacher called on her to conjugate the verb "to swim" in French, Lorena, still lost in her dream, said, "*Nado, nadas, nada, nadamos, nadan*"—the Spanish, not the French, conjugation.

During her last class, biology, Lorena overheard a group of whispering girls. One said, "Eddie and Lorena . . . I think they're stuck on each other."

If only it were true, Lorena thought. She hugged herself and felt the warmth of the jacket. For a moment, the beach scene replayed itself in the back of her mind.

The biology teacher made them cut apart dead frogs. He had been telling them for weeks that they would be dissecting a frog and that they should get used to the idea. He had said that dissecting a frog was no different than cutting apart a barbecued chicken.

"Gross," several of the students said, twisting their faces into ugly knots of disgust.

It *was* gross, Lorena thought. She took the knife in her hand and pierced the skin with a quick jab. She was surprised the frog didn't jump up, open its eyes, look at her, and plead, "Cut it out!"

She removed Eddie's jacket because she didn't want to get blood or gook on it. She folded it and placed it on a chair. Then she returned to dissecting, her face souring when the frog's slit belly opened, revealing a tangle of intestines.

When the bell rang, Lorena tossed her half-skinned frog back
into a white pan and hurried out of the class. She always had
to hurry because the bus she caught for home left promptly ten
minutes after school let out. She had to hurry more than usual
that day because she had to stop in the office to pick up a release.
Her French teacher was taking them to see a movie the next week.

She picked up the form, then raced to board the bus that
stood idling in front of the school. The driver was reading a
newspaper. His coffee was up on the dash, growing cold.

Lorena waved out the window to Guadalupe, who rode
another bus. "I'll call you when I get home," she yelled at her
friend, who was pushing a boy who was trying to make her smell
his froggy hands.

Lorena found a seat. After a few minutes the driver folded his
newspaper, drank his coffee in three gulps, wiped his mouth on
his sleeve, and muttered, "Hang on."

The bus lurched and was coughing a black plume of smoke
when Lorena looked out the window and saw Eddie and his friend
Frankie stomping on milk cartons. An explosion of milk burst
into the air, scaring two girls who were standing nearby.

Lorena's hands went straight to her shoulders. "The jacket!" she
screamed. She shot from her seat and ran up the aisle to the driver.

"You've got to stop! I forgot Eddie's jacket!"

"Who's Eddie? I don't know no Eddie," the driver said,
shifting into third. "Sit down."

"I lost his jacket!" she screamed, stomping her foot like a little girl.

The driver downshifted as he came to a red light. He turned
to her, his lined face dark with stubble. He warned her again with
a wag of one ink-stained finger, "I said, sit down."

And she did. She returned to her seat and sat clutching her
books. "How can I ever tell Eddie?" she whimpered. She closed
her eyes and pictured herself telling him. He was standing by his
locker, trying to remember his combination. He wore a T-shirt, the
braille of goose bumps on his arms. Outside it was raining hard.

That was Wednesday afternoon. Lorena was frantic that evening when she spoke in hushed tones to Guadalupe on the telephone in the hallway at home.

"How could I be such a _mensa_?" she scolded herself as she sat cross-legged, the telephone cradled in one hand and a cookie in the other. She blamed her biology teacher for her problem. If he hadn't made them dissect frogs, she wouldn't have been so absentminded.

The next day Lorena rushed from the bus to the biology room. The jacket was not there.

"Darn it," she snarled, pounding her fist on a table. She turned angrily and shot a fiery glance at the frogs that had been tossed into the white pan to await first period.

She decided to keep her distance from Eddie by sneaking down the hallways pretending to be reading a book. She spent most of her break and lunch period in the rest room, brushing her hair and worrying. Now and then Guadalupe would come into the rest room to tell her where Eddie was and what he was doing. He had been slap-boxing with Frankie.

Lorena and Guadalupe decided to stay home Friday so that Lorena could avoid Eddie. She spent the day reading _Seventeen_ and eating bowls of saltless popcorn.

The girls decided that they would pool their money and go shopping on Saturday to replace the jacket. Lorena figured she had about eighty dollars, and with Guadalupe's thirty-four dollars, her life savings, they would have enough to buy a new Raiders jacket.

It had been rainy when Lorena awoke Saturday morning, and Guadalupe was really sick but still willing to go with her to Fashion Fair. ❷

"Mom," Lorena called as she walked into the kitchen. "It's

> ❷ **Identifying Main Idea and Supporting Details**
> What idea about Guadalupe do these details support?

Vo·cab·u·lary

mensa (MEN sah) fool (Spanish)

stopped raining."

"Did you clean your room?" her mother asked. She was sitting at the kitchen table cutting coupons from the *Fresno Bee* newspaper.

"Two times. I even cleaned the aquarium."

Her mother sighed as she stood. Peeking out the kitchen window, she saw that the rain had let up. It was still misty, but the skinny plum tree they had planted last winter was no longer wavering in the wind. Her mother said, "OK, but you don't have to get me anything fancy."

Lorena had told her mother she wanted to go shopping so that she could buy her a gift for her birthday, which was the next week.

They drove to pick up Guadalupe, who climbed into the car and immediately sneezed. She had a wad of crumpled Kleenex in her fist.

"Ay, I bet you got a cold from going outside with your hair wet," Lorena's mother said, accelerating slowly. She didn't want to chance running into a mailbox again.

"I caught a cold from my stupid brother," Guadalupe said. She turned to Lorena and, leaning into her shoulder, whispered, "I got ten more dollars."

They drove in silence to Fashion Fair.

"I don't want you two to fool around," Lorena's mother warned as she let the girls out. She tried to look serious, but both of them knew that she was a softy.

Lorena promised to behave. Guadalupe sneezed and said, "Thank you, Mrs. Rocha. I'll be sure that Lorena doesn't act up."

Lorena pushed Guadalupe, who laughed and said, "Well, *I* am older."

The Raiders Jacket

"But not wiser, _esa_."

The two girls watched the car pull away with Mrs. Rocha gripping the steering wheel with both hands. Then they walked into the mall and headed toward Macy's, which was at the other end. Guadalupe wanted to stop and buy an Orange Julius drink, but Lorena hissed, "Lupe, we may not have enough money!"

"Yeah, you're right," Guadalupe said, stopping to open her purse. She rifled through it—eyeliner, an old report card, gum, sticky Lifesavers, a scrap of paper with the phone number of a so-so-looking boy from Tulare. Her fingers at last squeezed the envelope that contained forty-four dollars. She looked around before handing the envelope to Lorena. "You can pay me back in a month, right?"

"I think I can," Lorena said, her eyes big with excitement. The envelope weighed a lot, and Lorena slipped it into her coat pocket. "Lupe, you're a real friend."

The girls hurried to Macy's, and Lorena thrust her hand into her pocket every now and then to be sure the envelope was still there. They rode the escalator to the second floor and headed for the men's department, where two salesmen were standing near the cash register. They were bent over with laughter, apparently cracking up from a joke. Except for three other shoppers, the department was empty. It was quiet, too, except for the thump of music from an overhead speaker.

Lorena wanted to go unnoticed. She didn't want the salesmen to help. She and Guadalupe slid past them without being seen and stopped at a rack of Raiders jackets.

"I don't know what size Eddie wears," Lorena said, placing one hand to her chin as she studied the jackets. She took one from the rack and tried it on. The sleeves came down over her hands. "This looks like the size."

"Are you sure?" Guadalupe asked.

Vo·cab·u·lary

esa (EH sah) casual way of saying "you" in Spanish, most commonly used in Mexico

"No," she said after a moment. She slipped out of the jacket and looked at the tag inside—size 36. "Guadalupe, try it on."

"Me?" Guadalupe said, pointing a finger tipped with a polished nail at herself.

Guadalupe was an inch taller and twenty pounds heavier than Lorena, a _gordita_ to a _flaca_. She slipped the jacket on, arms outstretched, and asked, "How does it look?"

Lorena squinted and remarked, "I don't know. But I think it's the same size as Eddie's." She scanned the other jackets on the rack. She had to be sure.

"Why don't you just tell Eddie the truth?" Guadalupe suggested. "Then he can get his own jacket."

"I'm gonna look like a fool," Lorena said. "I don't want him to know I lost his jacket." She clicked a fingernail against her front teeth and stared at the rack. She stared some more and then replaced the jacket. "I think it was a size 34."

She walked to the cash register with the size 34 jacket. The salesmen were no longer laughing. One was helping a woman who was complaining about a broken zipper, and the other was punching a number into the telephone. When the second salesman saw Lorena, he hung up and asked, "Will this be all?"

Vo·cab·u·lary

gordita (gor DEE tah) heavy girl (Spanish)
flaca (FLAH kah) thin girl (Spanish)

"Yeah," she said, her hands shaking. Lorena brought out the envelope and the money from her own purse.

The salesman smiled and said, "Nice jacket. For your boyfriend?" He wagged his head from side to side and smiled, showing his clean, white teeth.

Lorena paid and took the shopping bag from the salesman. "Let's get outta here," she whispered. The two girls rode the escalator down a level and headed for the perfume department, where they dabbed their wrists with the richness of love and passion. **3**

> **3 Skimming**
> How will Eddie find out the truth?

"My mom would like this," Lorena said of a perfume emblazoned with Liz Taylor's signature. "Too bad I don't have enough money."

Neither of the girls was in a good mood. Neither of them liked spending all their money, especially Lorena. She had been saving her money to buy a moped when she turned sixteen and could get her license. Now that dream—and the dream of running in slow motion on the beach with Eddie—was dead.

Lorena and Guadalupe left Macy's and were standing in front of Hickory Farms inhaling the smells of 63 different cheeses and meats when they heard Eddie's voice. They turned and saw Eddie and his friend Frankie, both of whom were devouring bags of popcorn.

"Hey, Lorena, how come you left my jacket in biology?" Eddie asked coolly after he cleared his throat of popcorn. "I thought you liked me."

Lorena nearly fainted. This wasn't a dream. It was a nightmare—in silver and black. Eddie was wearing his Raiders jacket and a sneer on his face.

"Eddie, your jacket," Lorena blurted. She reached out to touch it, but Eddie pulled away. He took a step back and then said to Frankie, "The janitor found my jacket."

"I can explain," Lorena pleaded. "I didn't want to get any frog on your jacket—" Lorena stopped in midsentence. The story sounded ridiculous.

All the while Guadalupe stood staring at her shoes. She saw that her white laces had turned gray and wet from the rain. Her eyes filled with tears for her friend.

"Just leave me alone, *esa*," Eddie said.

Frankie licked his lips and said, "How could you do this to *mi carnal*? Man, he was treating you nice, *loca*."

After Eddie and Frankie left, chewing their popcorn casually as camels, Lorena and Guadalupe found a quiet place for a good cry. Lorena's tears fell, as her father would say, *como gatos y perros*.

"Eddie will never like me," she sobbed.

"There are bigger fish," Guadalupe comforted her.

They cried into each other's coats, then wiped their eyes and dabbed the buds of their mouths with lipstick. They returned the jacket and bought Lorena's mother some meats and cheeses, not the romantic perfumes called Passion or Ecstasy that filled their noses when they thought of love. ○

Answering the BIG Question

As you do the following activities, consider the Big Question:
When is the price too high?

WRITE TO LEARN Think about the options Lorena had when she discovered she had left the jacket behind. Write a brief entry in your Learner's Notebook about what Lorena could have done to make things turn out differently.

LITERATURE GROUPS Get together with two or three other students who have read "The Raiders Jacket." Come up with a new ending for the story based on what could have happened if Lorena had told Eddie the truth about his jacket.

Vo·cab·u·lary

mi carnal (mee kar NAHL) my buddy (Spanish)
loca (LOH kah) crazy girl (Spanish)

THE MONKEY'S PAW

by W.W. Jacobs
Dramatized by Harriet Dexter

What happens when a man gets a magical monkey's paw and ignores warnings not to use it—not just once, but three times?

Characters ❶

Mrs. White

Mr. White

Sergeant-Major Morris

Herbert White

Caller

> **❶ Previewing**
> Reading the list of characters and the scene settings before you read the play will help you to understand it better.

Setting

Scene 1

Time: About 1870

Setting: The living room of the Whites' modest cottage, in a
rural area of England. Two or three easy chairs are near the
fireplace at right. A rocking chair with knitting basket beside
it is nearby. A table holding a tea service is near the easy
chairs. A coat rack with a few <u>wraps</u>, including the Sergeant-
Major's raincoat and hat, is up left center, with umbrellas in
an umbrella stand beside it. Door to kitchen is down right,
door to outside is down left. A curtained window is in left
wall, and a few stairs up left lead to the upstairs.

At rise: Mr. White and Sergeant-Major Morris sit near the
fireplace. Morris holds a teacup which he fills from time to
time. Herbert stands near Mrs. White, who is in a rocking
chair, knitting. Rain is heard throughout the entire scene.

Mr. White. *(admiringly)* You certainly brought a <u>fund</u> of
interesting tales home from India, Morris.

Mrs. White. I should think you'd find it rather dull back in
England.

Morris. No, Mrs. White, I'm happy to be retired. Thirty years
in the army is a long time. Always an honor to serve Her
Majesty, of course, but nothing compares with one's native
land.

Mr. White. We're fortunate that you took the cottage down the
road. *(smiles at* Mrs. White) My wife has been fretting about
the loneliness.

Mrs. White. *(frowning)* We're so out of the way here. Seems as if
we've been forgotten by the authorities. *(nods toward outside)*
When it rains like this, the pathway's a bog, and the road's a
torrent.

Vo•cab•u•lary

wraps (raps) outerwear, such as coats or jackets
fund (fund) supply

Herbert. *(laughing)* You'll make the Sergeant-Major sorry he ever returned, Mother.

Morris. No danger of that. I'm enjoying the peace and quiet.

Herbert. You certainly didn't lack excitement in India. *(wistfully)* Sometimes I wonder if I'll be making farm machinery for the rest of my life.

Morris. Stick to your job at the factory, Herbert. Better off in the long run.

Mr. White. I know how Herbert feels. I'd like to visit India myself. I've heard so much about those temples . . . and the jugglers and snakecharmers.

Herbert. *(eagerly)* Didn't you mention a rather remarkable monkey's paw, or something of the sort last week, Sergeant-Major? (Mr. *and* Mrs. White *lean forward with anticipation.*)

Morris. *(uncomfortably)* It was nothing. At least, nothing worth hearing.

Mrs. White. *(grinning)* You can't stop now, Morris.

Morris. *(offhandedly)* Oh, it's just what you might call a bit of magic. (Whites *watch with rapt attention as he fumbles in his pocket.*) Nothing but an ordinary little paw dried to a mummy. ❷ *(takes a black, shriveled object from pocket)*

Mrs. White. *(recoiling)* Ugh—nasty!

Herbert. *(taking paw and examining it)* It really is a monkey's paw! *(hands it to Mr. White)*

Mr. White. What's so special about it?

Morris. A very old fakir—a holy man—put a spell on it. He wanted to show that fate rules people's lives and those who interfere with fate do so to their sorrow.

> ❷ **Scanning**
> Scan the rest of the scene—what is the mood that surrounds the monkey's paw?

Vo•cab•u•lary

recoiling (rih KOYL ing) shrinking away in fear and disgust

Mr. White. What is the spell?

Morris. Three different men may have three wishes on the paw. (Mrs. White *laughs nervously.*)

Herbert. (*grinning with disbelief*) Did you have three, sir?

Morris. (*somberly*) I did.

Mrs. White. And were they granted?

Morris. They were. The man who owned the paw before me had his three wishes. I don't know what the first two were, but his wife told me (*pauses impressively*) the third was for death. (Mrs. White *gasps.* Mr. White *goes to her, smiling reassuringly.*)

Herbert. If you've already had your three, sir, the paw is no good to you, so why do you keep it?

Morris. (*shrugging*) I thought of selling it, but it has caused enough mischief already. Besides, I don't think people would buy it. Many think it's a fairy tale, and the others want to try it first and pay me afterward.

Mr. White. If you could have another three wishes, would you?

Morris. No. (He *suddenly takes the paw from* Mr. White *and throws it into the fire. The others are startled.*)

Mr. White. (*grabbing paw from the fire*) Why did you do that?

Morris. Better let it burn!

Mr. White. If you don't want it, Morris, give it to me.

Morris. You can keep it, but don't blame me for what happens!

Mrs. White. (*shuddering*) I don't like it, dear.

Herbert. I say let's keep it. What harm can come, whether it's a fairy tale or not?

Mr. White. (*staring at the paw, fascinated*) How do you make the wish?

Morris. (*sighing resignedly*) Hold it up in your right hand and wish aloud. But I warn you of the consequences.

Mrs. White. (*crossing to table*) I'm going to clear the dishes, and if you're determined to make a wish, Father, you can wish for two more pairs of arms for me! (Herbert *and* Mrs. White *laugh*

as Mr. White holds paw up in his right hand. Morris leaps at him with a cry of alarm and knocks his arm down.)

Morris. If you must wish, wish for something sensible!

Mr. White. *(sheepishly)* I was just having a bit of fun, Morris. I wouldn't wish for anything <u>frivolous</u>.

Morris. Best not to wish at all! The results can be disastrous. ❸ *(slowly)* And what happens seems so natural you might attribute it to coincidence.

Mrs. White. *(soothingly)* If it will ease your fears, Sergeant-Major, I can't think of anything we'd wish for.

Morris. But the temptation will remain as long as you own the paw. *(sighs)* I wish

> ❸ **Identifying Main Idea and Supporting Details** What details have you seen so far that support Morris's opinion of the monkey's paw?

Vo•cab•u•lary

frivolous (FRIV uh lus) silly; not useful

I'd kept quiet about it. (*He rises.*)

Herbert. You're not going, are you, sir? It's still early.

Morris. Better to start now before the storm worsens.

Herbert. (*bringing* Morris's *hat and coat*) I'll be happy to walk part of the way with you.

Mr. White. (*quickly*) I'll do it, Herbert. I need some exercise, anyway. (*He ignores* Morris's *protests and gets his coat and umbrella.*)

Mrs. White. Goodnight, Sergeant-Major.

Herbert. (*smiling*) Don't worry about the monkey's paw, sir. I think you'll find us safe and sound the next time you come.

Morris. (*solemnly*) I hope so, Herbert. (*shaking hands*) Until next week, then. (*He follows* Mr. White *out.*)

Mrs. White. (*returning to her dishes*) Such an interesting man. What do you make of that story about the monkey's paw, Herbert?

Herbert. (*laughing*) I'd say there's as much truth to that as there is in the rest of his tales. The Sergeant-Major has a lively imagination. (Mrs. White *laughs and takes dishes to kitchen.* Herbert *goes to mantel, takes paw, and is idly examining it when* Mr. White *returns.*) Back already? (Mr. White *enters.*)

Mr. White. (<u>*evasively*</u>, *as he hangs up his coat*) Morris didn't want me to accompany him. He thinks I'm not as used to foul weather as he is.

Mrs. White. (*eyeing him shrewdly*) The truth, Father. How much did you give him for the monkey's paw? ❹

Mr. White. (*guiltily*) A <u>trifle</u>. He didn't want it. Told me again to throw the thing away.

Herbert. (*laughing*) You're not likely to do

> ❹ **Scanning**
> Scan the rest of the scene to find out what Mr. White wished for.

Vo•cab•u•lary

evasively (ih VAY siv lee) in a purposely vague way
trifle (TRY ful) small amount

that, after paying for it. (*with a sly glance at* Mrs. White) Better wish to be an emperor, Father. Then you won't be henpecked.

Mrs. White. (*pretending to be shocked*) Better wish for a more respectful son! (*as* Mr. White *takes paw from mantel and looks at it thoughtfully*) What are you doing with that?

Mr. White. Wondering what I should wish for. It seems to me I have all I want.

Mrs. White. (*promptly*) Then it's best not to wish. You heard what the Sergeant-Major said. Why tempt fate?

Herbert. Wouldn't you be happy if you could pay off the mortgage, Father? It would only take two hundred pounds.

Mr. White. (*slowly*) Why, yes, Herbert. That would be a great help. (*He glances questioningly at* Mrs. White. *She shrugs, goes to her rocking chair and takes up her knitting. Hesitantly.*) Should I, Herbert?

Herbert. Of course! You know you're keen on it, and you have nothing to lose. (*as his parents look at him sharply*) I think that's all bosh—about tempting fate.

Mr. White. (*holding up paw and clearing his throat self-consciously*) I wish for two hundred pounds! (*Instantly he cries out and drops the paw.* Herbert *hurries to his side and* Mrs. White *rises in alarm.*)

Herbert. What is it, Father?

Mrs. White. Why did you do that?

Mr. White. (*recoiling from the paw*) It twisted in my hands like a snake—just as I made the wish!

Mrs. White. You must have fancied[1] it.

Mr. White. I didn't fancy it! Gave me quite a shock.

Herbert. Well, I don't see the money. (*He picks up paw and puts it on mantel.*)

Mr. White. You're not likely to see the money yet. Remember what Morris said! It'll come about in such an unexpected way,

....

[1]Fancied here means "imagined."

we'll put it down to coincidence.

Herbert. *(grinning)* Then I shan't stand about and wait. I have a job to go to in the morning, you know. *(starting toward stairs)* I expect you'll find the cash in a big bag on your bed, and a horrible goblin watching as you open it.

Mr. White. *(uneasily)* I wouldn't <u>jest</u> about it, Herbert.

Mrs. White. Perhaps Herbert is right, Father. We should treat this whole episode as a prank. Anyhow, even if we did get the two hundred pounds, how could it hurt us?

Herbert. It could drop on Father's head from the sky. *(He laughs, kisses his mother, and exits upstairs. Mr. White is staring at the paw with a troubled expression.)*

Vo•cab•u•lary

jest (jest) joke around

The Monkey's Paw

Mrs. White. (*putting a hand on his arm*) Tomorrow will bring sunny skies, and all this turmoil about the monkey's paw will seem nothing but foolishness.

Mr. White. Perhaps.

Mrs. White. We'd best get to bed. (*She waits a moment, but Mr. White shows no inclination to leave. She shakes her head and exits upstairs. Mr. White slowly crosses to the mantel, as though against his will, picks up the paw and stares at it with growing repugnance. Then he quickly replaces it on mantel and goes upstairs. Curtain.*)

Setting

Scene 2

Time: The next afternoon.

Setting: Same as Scene 1.

At rise: The curtains are open and sunshine streams through the windows. Mrs. White is dusting the furniture and Mr. White enters from kitchen.

Mrs. White. Finished your gardening?

Mr. White. (*nodding*) Herbert will be happy to know the green beans are coming up nicely. He's so partial to them. (*smiles faintly*) Perhaps we should use the two hundred pounds for a really fine vegetable garden . . . one that will take care of itself.

Mrs. White. (*laughing*) We won't see any two hundred pounds. I'm convinced that ugly little paw has no magic powers, and it doesn't look very sinister in the light of day.

Mr. White. I'm not so sure of that.

Mrs. White. Why, Herbert saw through that story at once. Remember his funny remarks?

Mr. White. (*nodding*) I expect he'll have even funnier things to

---

Vo·cab·u·lary

repugnance (rih PUG nuns) strong dislike

say about it when he gets home this evening. (*darkly*) But for all that, the thing did move in my hand. That I'll swear to.

Mrs. White. (*mildly*) You thought it did.

Mr. White. It did. There was no thought about it. I had just— (*He stops as* Mrs. White *suddenly looks toward the window.*) What's the matter?

Mrs. White. I heard something. (*puts dustcloth into her pocket and crosses to window*) Yes. Someone is coming toward the gate. (*she peers out as* Mr. White *joins her.*) Do you know that man?

Mr. White. (*looking*) I'm not likely to know anyone who wears a silk hat. Not that it matters. I think he's leaving.

Mrs. White. (*perplexed*) But he started to open the gate. He can't seem to make up his mind. (*Sound of gate clanging shut is heard offstage.*) Here he comes! (*She hurriedly takes off apron and puts it under the rocking chair cushion. She smoothes her hair as knock is heard at the door.* Mr. White *opens door to* Caller.)

Mr. White. Good morning, sir. (*motions* Caller *in; sociably*) Not really morning anymore. I finished my gardening half an hour ago and it was just going on noon then. (*pauses uncertainly as* Caller *remains just inside door, twisting his hat in his hands*)

Mrs. White. (*coming forward*) Is there something we can do for you, sir?

Caller. I was asked to call. (*nervously*) I'm from Mark and Meggins. (Mr. *and* Mrs. White *look at one another apprehensively.*)

Mrs. White. (*tremulously*) **5** Has something happened to Herbert? (*When the* Caller *does not respond she panics.*) What is it?

Mr. White. (*putting his arm around*

> **5 Using Text Structures**
> How does the use of question-and-answer here heighten the mood?

Vo•cab•u•lary

perplexed (pur PLEKSD) puzzled
apprehensively (ap rih HEN siv lee) fearfully; uneasily
tremulously (TREM yoo lus lee) in a trembling, quivering way

her) There, Mother, don't jump to conclusions. (*to* Caller, *beseechingly*) You've not brought bad news, have you?

Caller. (*averting his face*) I'm sorry.

Mrs. White. Is he hurt? Tell us, is he hurt?

Caller. (*softly*) Badly hurt. (*as* Mrs. White *cries out*) But he is not in any pain.

Mrs. White. Oh, thank God for that! Thank God— (*She breaks off with a gasp as his meaning dawns on her, and turns blindly to her husband, who grasps her hand.*)

Caller. It was an accident . . . with the machinery. (Mr. *and* Mrs. White *stare at him.*)

Vo•cab•u•lary

beseechingly (bih SEECH ing lee) in an earnest or begging manner
averting (uh VURT ing) turning away

Mr. White. *(tonelessly)* The machinery. *(after a pause)* He was the only one left to us. It is hard.

Caller. *(going to window and looking out)* The firm wished me to convey their sincere sympathy to you. *(miserably)* I beg you to understand that I am only their servant, and merely obeying orders.

Mrs. White. *(dully)* Yes. Obeying orders.

Caller. I was to say that Mark and Meggins disclaims all responsibility. But in consideration of your son's services, they wish to present you with a certain sum as compensation. *(Mr. and Mrs. White stare at him in growing horror.)*

Mr. White. *(barely audible)* How much?

Caller. *(taking an envelope from his coat)* Two hundred pounds. *(Mrs. White screams and her husband catches her as she sways. Quick curtain.)*

Setting

Scene 3

Time: One week later. Night.

Setting: The same.

At rise: The stage is dimly lit. Mrs. White, who is in her nightclothes, is huddled in a chair, sobbing. After a moment, Mr. White, in robe and slippers, and holding a candle or kerosene lamp, comes down the stairs. He pauses for a moment at foot of stairs, sadly regarding his wife, then places candle on table and goes to her.

Mr. White. *(tenderly)* Come back to bed. You will be cold here.

Mrs. White. It is colder for my son! *(She sobs.)*

Mr. White. *(trying to coax her to get up)* He has been gone for a week. Your tears cannot bring him back.

Mrs. White. *(lashing out at him)* He was all we had! When we lost the other children I promised myself I would never let anything happen to Herbert! *(rises and pounds him with her fists)* Why did you make that wish? The wish that killed him!

Mr. White. (*catching her hands*) Do you think I have not asked myself that same question ever since his death? I will never know a peaceful moment until I am laid in the ground beside him!

Mrs. White. (*collapsing against him*) Forgive me. You are no more to blame than I am. I should have stopped you. The Sergeant-Major warned us. (*She cries bitterly.*)

Mr. White. Poor Morris. He is suffering almost as much as we are.

Mrs. White. I know he is. But I wish we had never met him! I wish we had never heard of the monkey's paw! (*She clings to him, weeping helplessly for a moment, then suddenly stiffens. She pulls away from her husband, her eyes blazing with excitement.*) The monkey's paw!

Mr. White. (*startled*) What? (*looking about frantically*) Where?

Mrs. White. Why didn't I think of it before? (*shaking him*) Get it! (*shouting*) Get it quickly! (*seeing his distracted expression*) You haven't destroyed it, have you?

Mr. White. No. I—I've hidden it. Why?

Mrs. White. (*ecstatically*) Don't you understand? We're saved! I just now thought of it!

Mr. White. (*frightened*) Thought of what?

Mrs. White. The other two wishes! We've only had one!

Mr. White. (*fiercely*) Was one not enough?

Mrs. White. No! We'll have one more! (*pushing him*) Get the monkey's paw and wish our boy alive again!

Mr. White. You are mad! Go back to bed—you don't know what you are saying!

Mrs. White. (*shouting*) Get it! Hurry!

Mr. White. (*shouting*) Didn't you hear what Morris said? We interfere with fate at our peril!

Vo•cab•u•lary

ecstatically (ek STAT ik lee) in a very happy or delighted way

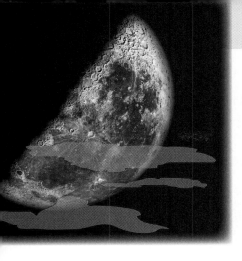

Mrs. White. (*raging at him*) We have already interfered with fate and lost our son! Now we shall have him back! Get the monkey's paw! (*She watches breathlessly as Mr. White stumbles to the umbrella stand, reaches in and pulls out the paw.*) Now— make the wish!

Mr. White. (*staring at paw, and whispering*) I don't want to see him. I'm afraid.

Mrs. White. What are you muttering about? Make the wish!

Mr. White. (*pleading*) Leave him in the grave, Mother. Let him rest.

Mrs. White. (*rushing at him*) Wish!

Mr. White. (*slowly, fearfully holding up the paw*) I wish my son alive again. (*His arm twitches violently, and he cries out as the paw flies out of his hand. He sinks, trembling, into a chair as Mrs. White runs to the window and parts the curtains. She stands at the window and stares out into the darkness, as though in a trance. After a moment, Mr. White joins her.*) Don't stay here. You must sleep. (*She pulls her hand away without looking at him.*) This cannot help us. It can only hurt us further. (*She does not respond and he shakes his head in defeat.*) Good night, then. (*He starts upstairs, and suddenly Mrs. White turns sharply.*)

Mrs. White. What was that? That creaking sound?

Mr. White. Nothing. A rat inside the walls. (*Mrs. White turns back to window and a moment later a single knock is heard at the door. Mr. White freezes on the stairs, and Mrs. White turns to look at the door. The knock is repeated, louder. A third, imperative knock brings Mr. White down the stairs as Mrs. White rushes to the door.*)

Vo·cab·u·lary

imperative (im PAIR uh tiv) commanding

Mrs. White. It's Herbert!

Mr. White. (*trying to hold her*) What are you going to do?

Mrs. White. (*struggling against him*) My boy is out there! Let me go!

Mr. White. You mustn't! It will destroy us!

Mrs. White. Let me go! I must open the door!

Mr. White. Whatever it is out there, don't let it in!

Mrs. White. (*blazing at him*) You're afraid of your own son! (*As Mr. White tries to pull her away from the door, she screams over her shoulder.*) I'm coming, Herbert! I'm coming! (*She finally breaks away and reaches the door, but she is unable to pull back the bolt. As she struggles with it, Mr. White begins searching the floor frantically for the paw.*) Help me! I can't open the door!

Mr. White. No! Leave it closed! (*A sudden, strong knock is heard, quickly followed by more. The knocking builds until it reaches a crescendo that <u>reverberates</u> through the room. Mrs. White manages to free the bolt and pull the door open. A howling rush of wind is heard.*)

Mrs. White. I'm here, Herbert! I'm here! (*She rushes out, just as Mr. White finds the paw. He scrambles to his feet, and at the same moment Mrs. White's terrified scream is heard offstage. She screams again and stumbles into the house. Mr. White slams and bolts the door.*) No! No! (*Mr. White holds her.*) Don't let me see him again! His face— (*The knocking begins again. It becomes louder and louder, threatening to break down the door. Mr. White supports his wife with one arm, and with the other hand holds the monkey's paw high.*)

Mr. White. (*shouting over the din*) I wish my son back in his grave—at peace forever! (*The knocking ceases. Mrs. White collapses in chair, and Mr. White hurls the monkey's paw into the fireplace. He grimly strikes a match as the curtain closes.*) ○

Answering the BIG Question

As you do the following activities, consider the Big Question:
When is the price too high?

WRITE TO LEARN Think about how Morris warned against wishing on the monkey's paw. Write a brief entry in your Learner's Notebook describing what you think he would say if he learned about Mr. White's three wishes.

LITERATURE GROUPS Meet with two or three others who have read "The Monkey's Paw." Discuss how the story illustrates the saying, "Be careful what you wish for."

Vo·cab·u·lary

reverberates (rih VUR buh rayts) echoes repeatedly

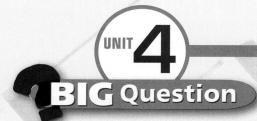

BIG Question

What do you do when you don't know what to do?

You're the only passenger in a small plane, and the pilot is sick. Hostile soldiers threaten the house you're staying in. What do you do? The characters in the selections face these and other difficult situations, and they must answer the question: **What do you do when you don't know what to do?**

As you read the selections in this unit, apply these reading skills.

- **Connecting** Link what you read to events in your own life or to other selections you've read.
- **Evaluating** Decide what you think about characters or real people in a selection. Make a judgment about the information in a text or about the author's craft.
- **Interpreting** Use your own understanding of the world to decide what the ideas in a selection mean.
- **Monitoring Comprehension** Pause from time to time to make sure you understand what you are reading.

HONOR THY FATHER

by Mark Stewart

from *Dale Earnhardt Jr.*

Dale Earnhardt Jr. struggles to overcome his grief over the death of his father in order to race again.

The death of Dale Earnhardt Sr. cast a shadow over the entire season. He had become the sport's most popular personality and its most beloved driver. Fans had just gotten used to the idea that the Earnhardts would be putting on an unforgettable father-son performance for years to come. Then he was gone, just like that. Dale Jr. decided to keep racing, hoping that focusing on his work would ease the grief and the pain. **①**

The following week, after the funeral and memorial service, Dale Jr. qualified for the Kmart/Dura Lube 400. Climbing

① Connecting
What do you do when you want to get your mind off your troubles?

behind the wheel on race day was the hardest thing Dale Jr. ever had to do—especially after a moving pre-race ceremony honoring his father. In no shape to drive a car at 200 mph (322 kph), he crashed on the first lap.

Dale Jr. fell into a deep depression after that. He continued to compete, but his heart was no longer in it. Sometimes, it was tough just waking up in the morning. Instead of finding it easier to cope with his dad's death, it seemed to get harder and harder. Months passed, and nothing changed. July 4 loomed on the horizon—the day the Winston Cup would return to Daytona for the Pepsi 400. Dale Jr. dreaded the thought of competing on the same track that had taken his father's life; the mere thought sent chills down his spine.

When he and his team arrived at the Daytona International Speedway, however, a different feeling came over him. Whenever he got behind the wheel, Dale Jr. swore he could sense his father's spirit. It was an uplifting experience, not a depressing one. On race day, he drove well for the first time in a long time, leading for more than 100 laps.

Fans kept their eyes glued to Dale Jr.'s number 8 car, wondering whether he could pull off a heart-wrenching victory. A 12-car pileup thinned out the field but left Dale Jr. in seventh place. Yet just when everyone was ready to write him off, he began to make up ground. He passed one car and then another. Soon he was within striking distance of the leaders.

The end of this race will be the subject of much debate, but the official results say Dale Earnhardt Jr. just blew everyone away. As he barreled into the lead, the other cars seemed to melt out of the way. "I have never been to a place where I was so dominant," he says.

When the checkered flag came down, there was not a dry eye in Daytona. What a perfect way to honor his father . . . and to shake off some of the demons that had been tormenting

Vo•cab•u•lary

loomed (loomd) seemed particularly difficult
tormenting (tor MENT ing) creating suffering in

him. Were his fellow drivers making room for him to pass out of respect for their fallen comrade? Or, as Dale Jr. claims, was his father there in the cockpit with him? **2**

2 Evaluating
What do you think about Dale Jr.'s claim?

Released from months of anguish, Dale Jr. cut loose on his way to Victory Lane, turning doughnuts on the infield, then climbing out onto his hood and thrusting his arms into the air in celebration. The roar of the crowd was deafening, and it got even louder when the other drivers hopped out of their cars and mobbed him. "I want to dedicate this one to my dad," he told everyone. "This one is for him!" ○

Answering the BIG Question

As you do the following activities, consider the Big Question:
What do you do when you don't know what to do?

WRITE TO LEARN Think about a time when you had to do something you really did not want to do. Write a brief entry in your Learner's Notebook describing how you dealt with the situation.

LITERATURE GROUPS Meet with two or three other students who have read "Honor Thy Father." Discuss other selections you have read recently in which a character or a real person had to overcome grief or fear.

from

HATCHET

by Gary Paulsen

Picture this: You're the only passenger in a small plane when something goes horribly wrong!

Brian Robeson stared out the window of the small plane at the endless green northern wilderness below. It was a small plane, a Cessna 406—a <u>bushplane</u>—and the engine was so loud, so roaring and consuming and loud, that it ruined any chance for conversation.

Vo•cab•u•lary

bushplane (BOOSH playn) a small private plane equipped to fly in and out of small woodland airports

Not that he had much to say. He was thirteen and the only passenger on the plane with a pilot named—what was it? Jim or Jake or something—who was in his mid-forties and who had been silent as he worked to prepare for take-off. In fact since Brian had come to the small airport in Hampton, New York to meet the plane—driven by his mother—the pilot had spoken only five words to him.

"Get in the copilot's seat."

Which Brian had done. They had taken off and that was the last of the conversation. There had been the initial excitement, of course. He had never flown in a single-engine plane before and to be sitting in the copilot's seat with all the controls right there in front of him, all the instruments in his face as the plane clawed for altitude, jerking and sliding on the wind currents as the pilot took off, had been interesting and exciting. But in five minutes they had leveled off at six thousand feet and headed northwest and from then on the pilot had been silent, staring out the front, and the drone of the engine had been all that was left. The drone and the sea of green trees that lay before the plane's nose and flowed into the horizon, spread with lakes, swamps, and wandering streams and rivers.

Now Brian sat, looking out the window with the roar thundering through his ears, and tried to catalog what had led up to his taking this flight.

The thinking started.

Always it started with a single word.

Divorce.

It was an ugly word, he thought. A tearing, ugly word that meant fights and yelling, lawyers—God, he thought, how he hated lawyers who sat with their comfortable smiles and tried to explain to him in legal terms how all that he lived in was coming apart—and the breaking and shattering of all the solid things. His home, his life—all the solid things. Divorce. A breaking word, an ugly breaking word.

Divorce.

Secrets.

No, not secrets so much as just the Secret. What he knew and had not told anybody, what he knew about his mother that had caused the divorce, what he knew, what he knew—the Secret. ❶

Divorce.

The Secret.

❶ **Monitoring Comprehension** What does the word *divorce* mean to Brian?

Brian felt his eyes beginning to burn and knew there would be tears. He had cried for a time, but that was gone now. He didn't cry now. Instead his eyes burned and tears came, the seeping tears that burned, but he didn't cry. He wiped his eyes with a finger and looked at the pilot out of the corner of his eye to make sure he hadn't noticed the burning and tears.

The pilot sat large, his hands lightly on the wheel, feet on the rudder pedals. He seemed more a machine than a man, an extension of the plane. On the dashboard in front of him Brian saw the dials, switches, meters, knobs, levers, cranks, lights, handles that were wiggling and flickering, all indicating nothing that he understood and the pilot seemed the same way. Part of the plane, not human.

When he saw Brian look at him, the pilot seemed to open up a bit and he smiled. "Ever fly in the copilot's seat before?" He leaned over and lifted the headset off his right ear and put it on his temple, yelling to overcome the sound of the engine.

Brian shook his head. He had never been in any kind of plane, never seen the cockpit of a plane except in films or television. It was loud and confusing. "First time."

"It's not as complicated as it looks. Good plane like this almost flies itself." The pilot shrugged. "Makes my job easy." He took Brian's left arm. "Here, put your hands on the controls, your feet on the rudder pedals, and I'll show you what I mean."

Brian shook his head. "I'd better not."

"Sure. Try it . . ."

Brian reached out and took the wheel in a grip so tight his knuckles were white. He pushed his feet down on the pedals. The plane slewed suddenly to the right.

"Not so hard. Take her light, take her light."

Brian eased off, relaxed his grip. The burning in his eyes was forgotten momentarily as the vibration of the plane came through the wheel and the pedals. It seemed almost alive.

"See?" The pilot let go of his wheel, raised his hands in the air and took his feet off the pedals to show Brian he was actually flying the plane alone. "Simple. Now turn the wheel a little to the right and push on the right rudder pedal a small amount."

Brian turned the wheel slightly and the plane immediately banked to the right, and when he pressed on the right rudder pedal the nose slid across the horizon to the right. He left off on the pressure and straightened the wheel and the plane righted itself.

"Now you can turn. Bring her back to the left a little."

Brian turned the wheel left, pushed on the left pedal, and the plane came back around. "It's easy." He smiled. "At least this part."

The pilot nodded. "All of flying is easy. Just takes learning. Like everything else. Like everything else." ❷ He took the controls back, then reached up and rubbed his left shoulder. "Aches and pains—must be getting old."

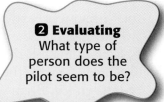

❷ **Evaluating**
What type of person does the pilot seem to be?

Brian let go of the controls and moved his feet away from the pedals as the pilot put his hands on the wheel. "Thank you . . ."

But the pilot had put his headset back on and the gratitude was lost in the engine noise and things went back to Brian looking out the window at the ocean of trees and lakes. The burning eyes did not come back, but memories did, came flooding in. The words. Always the words.

Divorce.

The Secret.

Fights.

Split.

The big split. Brian's father did not understand as Brian did, knew only that Brian's mother wanted to break the marriage apart. The split had come and then the divorce, all so fast, and the court had left him with his mother except for the summers and what the judge called "visitation rights." So formal. Brian hated judges as he hated lawyers. Judges that leaned over the bench and asked Brian if he understood where he was to live and why. Judges with the caring look that meant nothing as lawyers said legal phrases that meant nothing.

In the summer Brian would live with his father. In the school year with his mother. That's what the judge said after looking at papers on his desk and listening to the lawyers talk. Talk. Words.

Now the plane lurched slightly to the right and Brian looked at the pilot. He was rubbing his shoulder again and there was the sudden smell of body gas in the plane. Brian turned back to avoid embarrassing the pilot, who was obviously in some discomfort. Must have stomach troubles.

So this summer, this first summer when he was allowed to have "visitation rights" with his father, with the divorce only one month old, Brian was heading north. His father was a mechanical engineer who had designed or invented a new drill bit for oil drilling, a self-cleaning, self-sharpening bit. He was working in the oil fields of Canada, up on the tree line where the <u>tundra</u> started and the forests ended. Brian was riding up from New York with some drilling equipment—it was lashed down in the rear of the plane next to a fabric bag the pilot had called a survival pack, which had emergency supplies in case they had to make an emergency landing—that had to be specially made in the city, riding in a bushplane with the pilot named Jim or Jake or something who had turned out to be an all right guy, letting him fly and all. **3**

3 Monitoring Comprehension
What is the purpose of Brian's journey?

Except for the smell. Now there was a constant odor, and Brian took another look at the pilot, found him rubbing the shoulder and down the arm now, the left arm, letting go more gas and wincing. Probably something he ate, Brian thought.

His mother had driven him from the city to meet the plane at Hampton where it came to pick up the drilling equipment. A drive in silence, a long drive in silence. Two and a half hours of sitting in the car, staring out the window. Once, after an hour, when they were out of the city she turned to him.

"Look, can't we talk this over? Can't we talk this out? Can't you tell me what's bothering you?"

And there were the words again. Divorce. Split. The Secret. How could he tell her what he knew? So he had remained

Vo·cab·u·lary

tundra (TUN druh) A treeless plain in the Arctic

silent, shook his head and continued to stare unseeing at the countryside, and his mother had gone back to driving only to speak to him one more time when they were close to Hampton.

She reached over the back of the seat and brought up a paper sack. "I got something for you, for the trip."

Brian took the sack and opened the top. Inside there was a hatchet, the kind with a steel handle and a rubber handgrip. The head was in a stout leather case that had a brass-riveted belt loop.

"It goes on your belt." His mother spoke now without looking at him. There were some farm trucks on the roads now and she had to weave through them and watch traffic. "The man at the store said you could use it. You know. In the woods with your father."

Dad, he thought. Not "my father." My dad. "Thanks. It's really nice." But the words sounded hollow, even to Brian.

"Try it on. See how it looks on your belt."

And he normally would have said no, would normally have said no that it looked too hokey to have a hatchet on your belt. Those were the normal things he would say. But her voice was thin, had a sound like something thin that would break if you touched it, and he felt bad for not speaking to her. Knowing what he knew, even with the anger, the hot white hate of his anger at her, he still felt bad for not speaking to her, and so to humor her he loosened his belt and pulled the right side out and put the hatchet on and rethreaded the belt.

"Scootch around so I can see."

He moved around in the seat, feeling only slightly ridiculous.

She nodded. "Just like a scout. My little scout." And there was the tenderness in her voice that she had when he was small, the tenderness that she had when he was small and sick, with a cold, and she put her hand on his forehead, and the burning came into his eyes again and he had turned away from her and looked out the window, forgotten the hatchet on his belt and so arrived at the plane with the hatchet still on his belt.

Because it was a bush flight from a small airport there had

been no security and the plane had been waiting, with the engine running when he arrived and he had grabbed his suitcase and pack bag and run for the plane without stopping to remove the hatchet.

So it was still on his belt. At first he had been embarrassed but the pilot had said nothing about it and Brian forgot it as they took off and began flying.

More smell now. Bad. Brian turned again to glance at the pilot who had both hands on his stomach and was grimacing in pain, reaching for the left shoulder again as Brian watched.

"Don't know, kid . . ." The pilot's words were a hiss, barely audible. "Bad aches here. Bad aches. Thought it was something I ate but . . ."

He stopped as a fresh spasm of pain hit him. Even Brian could see how bad it was—the pain drove the pilot back into the seat, back and down.

"I've never had anything like this . . ." ❹

The pilot reached for the switch on his mike cord, his hand coming up in a small arc from his stomach, and he flipped the switch and said, "This is flight four six . . ."

> ❹ **Interpreting**
> What do you think is happening to the pilot?

And now a jolt took him like a hammerblow, so forcefully that he seemed to crush back into the seat, and Brian reached for him, could not understand at first what it was, could not know.

And then he knew.

Brian knew. The pilot's mouth went rigid, he swore and jerked a short series of slams into the seat, holding his shoulder now. Swore and hissed, "Chest! Oh God, my chest is coming apart!"

Brian knew now.

The pilot was having a heart attack. Brian had been in the shopping mall with his mother when a man in front of Paisley's store had suffered a heart attack. He had gone down and screamed about his chest. An old man. Much older than the pilot.

Brian knew.

The pilot was having a heart attack and even as the knowledge came to Brian he saw the pilot slam into the seat one more time, one more awful time he slammed back into the seat and his right leg jerked, pulling the plane to the side in a sudden twist and his head fell forward and spit came. Spit came from the corners of his mouth and his legs contracted up, up into the seat, and his eyes rolled back in his head until there was only white.

Only white for his eyes and the smell became worse, filled the cockpit, and all of it so fast, so incredibly fast that Brian's mind could not take it in at first. Could only see it in stages.

The pilot had been talking, just a moment ago complaining of the pain. He had been talking.

Then the jolts had come.

The jolts that took the pilot back had come, and now Brian sat and there was a strange feeling of silence in the thrumming roar of the engine—a strange feeling of silence and being alone. Brian was stopped.

He was stopped. Inside he was stopped. He could not think past what he saw, what he felt. All was stopped. The very core of him, the very center of Brian Robeson was stopped and stricken

with a white-flash of horror, a terror so intense that his breathing, his thinking, and nearly his heart had stopped.

Stopped.

Seconds passed, seconds that became all of his life, and he began to know what he was seeing, began to understand what he saw and that was worse, so much worse that he wanted to make his mind freeze again.

He was sitting in a bushplane roaring seven thousand feet above the northern wilderness with a pilot who had suffered a massive heart attack and who was either dead or in something close to a coma.

He was alone.

In the roaring plane with no pilot he was alone.

Alone. **5**

When the plane crashes, Brian survives. He is bruised, hungry, and thirsty—and alone. Somehow, he must figure out what to do to keep himself alive in the wilderness. To find out what happens to Brian, read the book Hatchet *by Gary Paulsen.* ○

> **5 Connecting**
> How do you think you would react in a situation like this?

Answering the BIG Question

As you do the following activities, consider the Big Question:
What do you do when you don't know what to do?

WRITE TO LEARN Think about the two problems Brian faces—a family problem and a life-threatening problem. In your Learner's Notebook, write a brief entry telling what you think he can do about each problem.

LITERATURE GROUPS Get together with two or three other students who have read this selection. Discuss what you think Brian will do after the plane crashes. What will he do to try to survive in the wilderness?

SCIENCE AND CRIME

by Robert Gardner
from *Crime Lab 101*

Find out what happens when a man is accused of shooting a fellow hunter.

A group of hunters, hiding in woods and thickets, waited for deer to appear within their gun sights. Suddenly, one of the hunters, Robert Perry, spied an approaching deer and fired. To his dismay, a fellow hunter, not the deer, fell in the nearby brush.

The bullet had killed him. In the course of the investigation that followed, the local sheriff persuaded the guilt-ridden and confused hunter to sign a confession of negligent homicide. Perry was certain that he had seen and fired at a deer, but he could not explain how the bullet had hit his friend. The sheriff, on the other hand, believed Perry to be an <u>overzealous</u> hunter who had caught a glimpse of what he *thought* was a deer and had fired instead at his friend.

Perry's lawyer believed that his client was innocent. However, lacking the evidence needed to convince a jury, he turned to Herbert Leon MacDonell, a well-known *criminalist*— someone who uses scientific techniques to investigate crimes. (He could have been called a forensic scientist as well—one who applies science to matters of law.) MacDonell asked to examine the gun and the fatal bullet. He noticed that the wadding, the paper used to pack the gunpowder firmly into the cartridge, was still attached to the slug that had killed the hunter. Normally, air rushing over the speeding bullet causes the wadding to fall off the bullet about two feet from the gun. Yet, the fatal bullet had traveled several hundred feet, which suggested that it had not moved fast enough for air to tear the wadding off. He also found small

Vo•cab•u•lary

overzealous (oh vur ZEL us) too eager

pieces of wood on the slug, and careful weighings revealed that about forty-five grains (nearly 14 percent) of the lead normally found in such a slug was missing.

MacDonell then conducted some tests. First, he fired Perry's gun a number of times and found that the wadding did indeed fall from the slug a short distance from the gun. Next, he visited the site where the shooting had taken place. There he found a mark on a tree trunk close to the point where the gun had been fired. The wood fibers found on the slug were similar to fibers taken from the scarred tree.

In testimony given at the trial, MacDonell argued that the slug, intended for the deer, had <u>ricocheted</u> off the marked tree, where it lost its high velocity, changed its direction, then struck the victim. How else could one explain the wood fibers on the slug, the attached wadding, and the fact that the mass of the slug was forty-five grains less than normal? The jury agreed. They found Perry not guilty. **❶** ○

> **❶ Monitoring Comprehension**
> How does MacDonell convince the jury that Perry is not guilty?

Answering the BIG Question

As you do the following activities, consider the Big Question:
What do you do when you don't know what to do?

WRITE TO LEARN MacDonell used scientific techniques to investigate the shooting. In your Learner's Notebook, write a brief entry about how using a scientific approach could help you in an area of your life.

PARTNER TALK Meet with another student who has read "Science and Crime." Discuss a situation in which you were falsely accused of doing something wrong. How did you handle the situation?

Vo•cab•u•lary

ricocheted (RIK uh shayd) struck and then bounced off a hard surface

DOLPHIN RESCUE

by Gail Hennessey

Hungry, lost, and far from home: How can these dolphins survive?

*E*ight hurricane victims were found swimming in the Gulf of Mexico recently. While scientists from the National Oceanic and Atmospheric Administration (NOAA) were conducting an aerial study to assess damage from Hurricane

Katrina, they spotted eight Atlantic bottle-nosed dolphins. The six females and two males were washed away from the Marine Life Oceanarium in Gulfport, Mississippi.

The dolphins were given up for lost after a forty-foot wave swept over their tank and carried them out to sea. After looking at the wreckage of the aquarium, owner Moby Solangi said it was a miracle that any of the dolphins made it through all the <u>debris</u> without injury.

Although the eight dolphins, ranging in age from four to forty, weren't housed together at the aquarium, they were found swimming together as a group.

They were a bit battered and bruised, but mostly undernourished. Because they have spent most of their lives in captivity at the aquarium (three of the dolphins were born there), they have no survival skills. They are used to being fed and do not know how to protect themselves from predators.

Rescue Mission

Marine trainers have been boating out to the dolphins to feed them. They are giving them fish with vitamins and medicines to fight infection.

"Their trainers from the Oceanarium have also been giving the dolphins badly needed TLC (tender loving care), talking with them, stroking them, and teaching them techniques to capture them," said Laura Engleby, a biologist at NOAA's Fisheries Service. "The trainers are conditioning the dolphins to beach themselves onto floating foam mats." ❶

Trainers whistled and banged buckets to let the dolphins know it was meal time. Dolphins Toni, Jackie, and Noah were the first to be <u>coaxed</u> onto a mat and loaded

> ❶ **Interpreting**
> What is likely to happen to the dolphins if the trainers don't rescue them?

Vo•cab•u•lary

debris (dih BREE) remains of something broken down or discarded
coaxed (kohkst) persuaded

onto stretchers. Kelly, Noah's mom, was caught soon after. The remaining dolphins, Tamara, Shelly, Jill, and Elijah, were rescued just before Hurricane Rita blew into the Gulf Coast on Tuesday, September 20.

The dolphins jumped onto the mats when called by their trainers. **2** Cranes then hoisted the 350-pound dolphins onto a rescue boat. Once they were back on land, a police escort led a specially equipped van to a local Holiday Inn, where the dolphins were placed in the facility's swimming pool as a temporary shelter.

> **2 Monitoring Comprehension**
> How did the trainers rescue the dolphins?

The US Navy delivered temporary saltwater pools to house the dolphins.

"It's important to understand that marine park animals depend on human care," Engleby told Scholastic News Online. "So many groups were involved in the efforts to quickly and safely capture them as soon as possible, showing compassion to help humans as well as these sea mammals in need of our help." ○

Answering the BIG Question

As you do the following activities, consider the Big Question:
What do you do when you don't know what to do?

WRITE TO LEARN Think about the dangers the dolphins faced when the hurricane swept them away. In your Learner's Notebook, write a brief entry telling why you think those dolphins needed a lot of "tender loving care."

PARTNER TALK Meet with a partner to discuss how people found solutions to the problems of catching and housing the dolphins. Talk about times when you have had to think fast and use unusual means to tackle a problem.

THE CALAMITY KIDS IN
THE TIME LOOP LOCKET!

by Jerzy Drozd and Sara Turner

Amy's wish to grow up too fast backfires in a big way.

WRITE TO LEARN
Amy calls on Will and Jacob when she gets into a jam. Write an entry in your Learner's Notebook telling who you turn to when you don't know what to do. Why did you choose this person?

History Repeating (Almost)

by Hope Anita Smith

What can a person do to break a chain of anger and hurt feelings?

Momma is trying to talk to me,
but there are so many words
swimming around in my brain
that I'm sure they will start to
leak out all over the floor if I let
any more come in.
So I walk out of the room.
I walk out the front door,
and I keep walking.

I am walking away from
all the things that are making me hurt.
All the things that are making me mad.
I am walking away
just like Daddy did.
I am leaving all my problems
behind
just like Daddy—
I stop.
Because
suddenly
I am seeing Momma's face
when Daddy left.
I turn back toward home. **1**
I don't stop until my arms are
wrapped around Momma's middle
and my "I'm sorrys" are lost in her lap.
My tears stain her sun-gold dress like
a sudden rain.
She lifts my head,
cups my face in her hands, and says,
"You just changed the course of history."
"How'd I do that, Momma?" I ask.
"You came back." ○

1 Interpreting
How do you think the speaker feels about his father?

Answering the BIG Question

As you do the following activities, consider the Big Question:
What do you do when you don't know what to do?

WRITE TO LEARN Have you ever wanted to walk away from your problems, as the speaker wants to do? What new problems did the father create by leaving the family? Answer these questions in a brief entry in your Learner's Notebook.

LITERATURE GROUPS Get together with two or three other students who have read "History Repeating (Almost)." Discuss whether the speaker's relationship with his mother is likely to change as a result of this incident.

TERROR
in the
NIGHT

by Lee Roddy
from *Cry of Courage*

At the end of the war between North and South, a girl faces a test of courage.

Terror in the Night

Emily sat on the edge of Julie's high bed and watched her choose clothes to wear the next day.

"Mama is certainly excited," Julie observed. "She expects Papa home shortly now that the war's over."

Emily didn't answer. She slid off the bed and walked to the window. A pale slice of moon cast a cold light over the plantation. The coldness matched Emily's own feelings. She couldn't believe it was over that quickly.

Suddenly, she saw shadows flickering in and out of the open spaces between the great trees that lined the long drive from the public road to the manor house. She whispered urgently, "Julie, come here!"

Julie hurriedly joined her at the window. The shadows under the trees turned into horsemen, riding fast toward the house.

"It's William and his friends," his sister Julie announced. "They're the only ones who would run horses that fast in poor moonlight."

Emily started to nod, then froze. The riders passed between a large, open space between the trees so the moon clearly showed six men. One of them carried a Union flag.

"Yankees!" Julie cried in alarm and dashed out of the room shouting, "Mama! Mama! Yankees are outside!" **1**

Emily followed her cousin into the hallway, where Aunt Anna was hurriedly leaving her room as her maid tried to help her struggle into a dressing gown.

1 Interpreting
Why is Julie frightened by the presence of Yankee soldiers?

"Are you sure?" Aunt Anna asked anxiously.

"Positive, Mama! Emily and I both saw them riding up the drive from the public road, heading straight here!"

"That's right," Emily declared firmly.

"What'll we do, Mama?"

Aunt Anna's hand trembled as she tied the belt around her gown. "I don't know! Oh, I wish your father were here!"

Soldiers could be heard stopping their horses at the front door. Someone pounded on the large door with what sounded like a musket butt.

"Open up!" a man's voice demanded loudly.

"Mama!" Julie cried. "We've got to do something!"

"I know, but I thought we would have more warning so that we could escape . . ."

"Open up, I say!" the voice demanded loudly.

"Open up, or we'll break it down!"

Emily felt sorry for her aunt, who struggled to make a decision.

"Ignore them!" she cried. "Maybe they'll go away." Her right hand flitted nervously to cover her mouth.

She turned to her personal servant, who stood in the doorway of the bedchamber, the whites of her eyes showing. "Flossie, don't just stand there! Get something to put against this door in case those devils break in!"

Flossie screeched in terror and fled wildly down the long hallway toward the back of the house, ignoring her mistress's orders to come back.

Aunt Anna turned to the girls. "Quickly, come with me!" She motioned frantically for them to enter her bedchamber.

"Last chance!" the voice called. The pounding on the door intensified. "We're going to burn this place down around your heads!"

Terror in the Night

Julie was about to slam the door while Emily looked around for something heavy that could be shoved up against it. Aunt Anna gasped, clutched at her chest, and collapsed in the rocker near the bed.

"She'll be all right," Julie assured Emily. "It's just one of her spells. But those terrible men . . . !" She jerked her head toward the soldiers. "Do you think they really would burn us out?"

Emily's mind spun wildly in a moment of indecision. Then she took a quick, deep breath. "I'll go down and talk to them."

"No, you musn't!" Julie cried.

"It'll be all right. I'll tell them where I'm from. They're Union men, so I know they're honorable."

"No, please don't! You know what could happen—"

"We can't chance having them burn this place!" Emily ignored her cousin's further protests and aunt's low moaning sounds. Emily raced down the stairs toward the door, now starting to splinter under heavy blows . . .

Emily cautiously opened the door, now badly scarred from the blows of the musket stock. She glimpsed the six troopers in their blue uniforms with the yellow <u>piping</u> of Union cavalrymen. One held the red, white, and blue flag Emily knew and had loved all her life. But she sucked in her breath at the sight of another soldier with a pitch pine torch sputtering in the night.

As she stepped out onto the porch between the stately white <u>Corinthian</u> columns, the men fell silent. Emily stopped by the new Confederate flag where it sagged against its staff on the nearest white column.

"She's just a girl," exclaimed the surprised young man who had been pounding on the door with the musket.

Vo•cab•u•lary

piping (PY ping) thin, decorative cord on a coat
Corinthian (kor IN thee un) decorated in a style of ancient Greece

"I am twelve," Emily announced with a calmness she did not feel. She boldly looked from one man to the other before focusing on the officer sitting on his horse ahead of the other five mounts.

"My name is Emily Lodge, and I'm from Illinois," she said, keeping her voice steady. "This is my uncle and aunt's home, but no one is here except my invalid aunt and my cousin Julie." ❷

❷ Interpreting Why does Emily tell the Union soldiers that she is from Illinois?

"You expect us to believe that?" the man with the torch swung it closer to cast a better light on her face. "We're going in and searching for weapons and food!"

"Sergeant," the youthful leader with lieutenant's bars on his uniform said tartly, "I'm in charge here."

Emily caught a low but <u>derisive</u> snicker from the older sergeant. She guessed he resented the officer in his late teens who had probably been elected to rank because of his popularity with the other men.

"We have no weapons," Emily explained, "and I have assured my relatives that Federal soldiers are gentlemen and will behave themselves accordingly."

The seargeant muttered, "Lieutenant, you're not going to believe her, are you?"

Annoyed, Emily snapped, "I am a Christian and would not lie to you. It seems to me, Sergeant, that you are talking mighty bravely with five armed men against two girls and a semi-invalid woman!"

The sergeant laughed. "You're a saucy one for a <u>Secessh</u> gal!"

Vo•cab•u•lary

derisive (dih RY siv) mocking
Secessh (SEE sesh) a nickname for people from states that seceded from the Union; short for "secessionist"

"I am not a secessionist!" Emily declared, her violet eyes burning into the offending speaker.

"No?" the sergeant growled. "Whatever you are, I'll bet you run when I burn this dirty old rag." He extended the torch toward the new Confederate flag.

Hot words leaped from the girl's mouth. "I heard how well your friends ran at <u>Manassas</u>, and I suspect you were a part of that, only you ran the wrong way!"

"Lieutenant, let's stop this talking and get on with it!" the sergeant roared.

The young officer shifted uneasily in the saddle.

Emily moved her gaze to him. "Sir, if you are in charge of these men, please be so kind as to lead them away from here at once. Your presence is causing my aunt great physical distress."

The lieutenant replied, "Your accent convinces me of the truth of your origin. However, my men and I are lost, hungry, tired, and apparently in the heart of Rebel country. Although I would like to honor your request, I'm sure you understand that we must take what we need as a necessity of war." **3**

3 Monitoring Comprehension
What does Emily ask the lieutenant to do? How does he reply to her request?

"Well said, Lieutenant," the sergeant exclaimed. "Now, stand aside, or we'll ride these horses right over you and into your big, fancy house!"

"That's enough, Sergeant!" the officer said firmly, apparently shamed into taking charge. "We'll just walk through and take what—"

He stopped at the sound of rapidly approaching hoofbeats. "Who's that?" he asked Emily.

"I have no idea . . ." She hesitated as a thought streaked into her mind. "Unless," she said slyly, "it's Confederate cavalry."

Vo•cab•u•lary

Manassas (muh NAS us) the site of two Civil War battles

From the road there came a high, wavering yell that made gooseflesh form on the girl's arms. While the sound still ripped the night's stillness to shreds, it was echoed by another similar cry from off to the right, across the nearest tobacco field.

The fearsome cry erupted again to be echoed from the tobacco field. The rapid sound of hoofbeats made the Union cavalrymen uneasy. They turned their horses toward the lane leading to the public road.

"Wait!" the sergeant exclaimed. "Lieutenant, that's only one, maybe two horses!"

The officer hesitated while Emily held her breath. "I believe you're right, Sergeant."

"'Course I am!" He again lifted the flame toward the Confederate flag.

"Wait!" The lieutenant's sharp order stopped the sergeant's arm short of the flag. "Listen!"

Emily heard it, too. It sounded like a couple of riders were cutting through the tobacco fields toward the barn. But there were also several other hoofbeats that could be heard drumming on the public road.

"There's a bunch of them coming!" the sergeant exclaimed. "Riding hard, too!"

The wild yells again splintered the night from both sides of the great house, making the back of Emily's neck crawl with fear. But this time the yells were echoed from the other horsemen thundering through the night.

The lieutenant raised his voice. "There are too many of them. Sergeant, lead off before we get trapped!"

A mighty sob of relief shook Emily's body as the six Federals raced back the way they had come. She sagged weakly against the door, not understanding what had happened, but murmuring a prayer of gratitude. **4** ○

4 Evaluating
What is your opinion of Emily's character?

Answering the BIG Question

As you do the following activities, consider the Big Question:
What do you do when you don't know what to do?

WRITE TO LEARN Think about how Emily's aunt and cousin reacted to the soldiers' threat. Write a brief entry in your Learner's Notebook telling how they answered the question of what to do. How did their reaction differ from Emily's?

PARTNER TALK Get together with a partner who has read this selection. Discuss how Emily must have felt while she was talking with the Union soldiers. Talk about times when you have felt similar emotions. What was the situation, and what did you do?

by Eleanor Farjeon

How can one person possibly do all the exciting things life offers?

There isn't time, there isn't time
    To do the things I want to do—
With all the mountain tops to climb
    And all the woods to wander through
And all the seas to sail upon,
    And everywhere there is to go,
And all the people, every one,
    Who live upon the earth to know.
There's only time, there's only time
    To know a few, and do a few,
And then sit down and make a rhyme
    About the rest I want to do. ○

Answering the BIG Question

As you do the following activities, consider the Big Question:
What do you do when you don't know what to do?

WRITE TO LEARN Think about all the things you'd like to do during your lifetime. In your Learner's Notebook, write a brief entry to tell what you can do to accomplish as many of those things as possible.

LITERATURE GROUPS Get together with a few other students who have read "There Isn't Time." Discuss activities that you think would enrich your lives. Express them as lines that could be added to the poem.

DO FINGERPRINTS LIE?

by Michael Specter

A detective challenges one of law enforcement's most important tools.

By the spring of 1998, Shirley McKie, once a promising young detective, had become an outcast among her colleagues in the Strathclyde Police in Scotland. A year earlier, she had been assigned to a murder case in which a woman was stabbed with a pair of sewing scissors. Within hours of the killing, a team of <u>forensic</u> specialists had begun working their way through the victim's house. Along with blood, hair, and fibers, the detectives found some unexpected evidence: one of the prints lifted from the room where the murder took place apparently matched the left thumb of Detective McKie.

Crime scenes are often contaminated by fingerprints belonging to police officers, and investigators quickly learn to eliminate them from the pool of suspects. But McKie said that she had never entered the house. Four experts from the Scottish Criminal Record Office—the agency that stores and identifies fingerprints for Scotland's police—insisted, however, that the print was hers. Though McKie held to her story, even her father doubted her. "I love my daughter very much," Iain McKie, who served as a police officer in Scotland for more than 30 years, told me later. "But when they said the print was Shirley's, I have to admit I assumed the worst. My entire career I had heard that fingerprints never lie."

Nobody actually suspected McKie of murder, and in fact the victim's handyman, David Asbury, was charged with the crime. The sole physical evidence against him consisted of two fingerprints—one of his, lifted from an unopened Christmas gift inside the house, and one of the victim's, found on a cookie tin in Asbury's home. The last thing prosecutors needed was for McKie to raise questions in court about the quality of the evidence. Yet McKie did just that—repeating under oath that she had never entered the house. Asbury was convicted anyway, but Scottish prosecutors were enraged by McKie's testimony. As far as they were concerned, McKie had not only lied; she had challenged one of the pillars of the entire legal system. Despite their victory in the murder trial, they charged McKie with lying under oath. **❶**

❶ Connecting
Have you ever been accused of doing something you didn't do?

Desperate, she went to the public library and searched the Internet for somebody who

Vo·cab·u·lary

forensic (for EN zik) associated with courtrooms

might help her. Among the names she came upon was that of Allan Bayle, a senior forensic official at New Scotland Yard and perhaps the United Kingdom's foremost fingerprint expert. He agreed to review the prints, and what he saw astonished him. "It was obvious the fingerprint was not Shirley's," Bayle told me. "It wasn't even a close call. She was identified on the left thumb, but that's not the hand the print was from. It's the right forefinger. But how can you admit you are wrong about Shirley's print without opening yourself to doubt about the murder suspect, too?" Bayle posted a comment on Onin.com, a Web site visited regularly by the world's fingerprint community. "I have looked at the McKie case," he wrote. "The mark is not identical. I have shown this mark to many experts in the UK, and they have come to the same conclusions."

Bayle's <u>assertion</u> caused a furor. He was threatened with disciplinary action, shunned by his colleagues, and, after a quarter century with the Metropolitan Police, driven from his job. But in the end, McKie was <u>acquitted</u>, and Bayle's statement helped challenge a system that until then had simply been taken for granted.

For more than a century, the fingerprint has been regarded as a symbol of truth, particularly in the courtroom. When a trained expert tells a judge and jury that prints found at a crime scene match those of the accused, his testimony often decides the case. The Federal Bureau of Investigation's basic text on the subject is titled *The Science of Fingerprints*, and science is what FBI officials believe fingerprinting to be; their Web site states that "fingerprints offer an infallible means of personal identification." The Bureau maintains a database that includes the fingerprints of

Vo•cab•u•lary

assertion (uh SUR shun) positive statement
acquitted (uh KWIT ud) found a person not guilty

more than 43 million Americans; it can be searched from police stations and properly equipped police cars across the country. Fingerprints are regularly used to resolve disputes, prevent forgeries, and identify the dead; they have helped send countless people to prison.

But is fingerprint identification science? Scientists generate hypotheses and test them to see if they make sense; in laboratories throughout the world, researchers spend at least as much time trying to disprove a theory as they do trying to prove it. Eventually, those ideas that aren't disproved are accepted. But fingerprinting was developed by the police, not by scientists, and it has never been subjected to rigorous analysis. Yet it was so widely accepted in American courts that until recently further research no longer seemed necessary and none of any significance had been completed. ❷

❷ **Monitoring Comprehension** Why have people raised doubts about the accuracy of fingerprint identification?

This is true of other kinds of forensic evidence, such as bite marks, fiber analysis, and lie-detector tests, as well. Although forensic evidence has proved particularly powerful with juries, it is particularly weak as a science. By the 1980s this kind of evidence—without any statistical grounding or rationale—was called junk science. With the problem growing out of control, the Supreme Court said in 1993 that federal judges had to decide whether to allow "experts" to testify and whether forensic techniques met the rules of science.

Handwriting evidence and hair identification were judged unscientific. Questions were raised about techniques for tracing a bullet back to a particular gun. It was inevitable that questions would eventually be raised about fingerprint evidence. In 1999, Robert Epstein, a public defender in Philadelphia, was the first to challenge it. The critical evidence in one of his cases

---

Vo•cab•u•lary

rationale (rash un AL) reasoning

consisted of two fingerprints lifted from a car used in a robbery. To prepare for the trial, FBI officials had sent the prints to agencies in all 50 states; roughly 20 percent of the agencies failed to identify the prints correctly. "After all this time, we still have no idea how well fingerprinting really works," Epstein said. "The FBI calls it a science. By what definition is it a science? Where are the <u>data</u>? Where are the studies? We know that fingerprint examiners are not always right. But are they usually right or are they sometimes right? That, I am afraid, we *don't* know. Are there a few people in prison who shouldn't be? Are there many? Nobody has ever bothered to try and find out."

In 2002, Louis Pollak, a well-respected federal judge, held a hearing to determine whether to allow fingerprint experts to testify in a case being tried before him—a drug-related murder in Philadelphia. For three days, several of the world's most prominent experts argued about the reliability of fingerprints in his courtroom. The FBI's Stephen Meagher testified that no Bureau analyst had ever misidentified a person in court, and that the Bureau tested its analysts each year to see whether they correctly matched prints.

But Allan Bayle, the British forensic specialist who helped Shirley McKie, had a different view. He told the judge that the FBI's test was so easy that it could be passed with no more than six weeks of training. "If I gave my experts [at Scotland Yard] these tests, they would fall about laughing," he told the judge. Later, in a conversation with me, he pointed out that the fingerprints used in the tests were so different from each other that almost anybody could tell them apart. "Let's say I asked you to look at a zebra, a giraffe, an elephant, and a lion. Then I asked you to find the zebra. How hard would that be? What the Bureau should be doing is comparing five zebras and selecting among them." Bayle and other critics stopped short of calling fingerprint evidence junk science, but they noted that there are few data showing how often partial prints are properly identified.

Vo•cab•u•lary

data (DAY tuh or DAT uh) facts and information

Pollak decided to permit FBI fingerprint experts to testify, but only in this particular case. In an interview after his decision, he told me, "Other lawyers in fingerprint situations are now almost duty bound to raise these questions and challenges again. This decision is certainly not the end. I think we can be certain of that."

Although Shirley McKie, the Scottish detective, was acquitted of lying to the court, she felt unwelcome on the police force after her trial for <u>perjury</u> and resigned soon after. She never returned to work. Today she spends much of her time trying to force Scottish authorities to admit that what they did to her was wrong. "I believe a person made a mistake, and instead of admitting it they were prepared to send me to jail," Shirley McKie said after she was acquitted. "It ruined my life, and now I am trying to pick up the pieces."

The life of Allan Bayle, the man who came to her defense, has also changed. He now works as an independent consultant. Although he has been portrayed as a critic of fingerprint analysis, he is critical only of the notion that it should never be questioned. "It's a valuable craft," he said. "But is it a science like physics or biology? Well, of course not. All I have been saying is, let's admit we make errors and do what we can to eliminate them." **3**

> **3 Evaluating**
> Do you agree that fingerprint analysis is not a science? Why or why not?

Vo•cab•u•lary

perjury (PUR juh ree) lying under oath

Fingerprint Facts

The patterns on fingertips are more like handwriting than like a bar code. They can be so similar that even the most sophisticated computer program can't tell them apart; it takes a trained human eye to detect the subtle differences.

No two people—not even identical twins—have ever been shown to share fingerprints. The ridges that cover the skin on your hands and feet are formed by the 17th week in the womb; at birth they have become so deep that nothing can alter them, not even surgery. Some people have fingertips that are dominated by "loops," others by "arches," or small circles that examiners call "lakes," or smaller ones still, called "dots." Together these details are referred to as minutiae—an average human fingerprint may contain as many as 150 minutiae points. To identify fingerprints, an expert must compare these points individually, until enough of them correspond that he or she feels confident of a match.

When fingerprints are properly recorded (inked, then rolled, finger by finger, onto a flat surface), identification works almost flawlessly. The trouble is that investigators in the field rarely see clean prints that can be quickly analyzed by a computer; most of the prints introduced at criminal trials are fragments known as partial prints. Crime scenes are messy, and the average fingerprint taken from them represents only a fraction of a full fingertip—about 20 percent. Even that fraction is often distorted and hard to read, having been lifted from a grainy table or a bloodstained floor.

The technology for retrieving partial and latent (invisible) fingerprints keeps improving. In order to find difficult prints on an irregular surface, such as the human body, crime-scene investigators blow fumes of superglue over it. As the fumes adhere to the surface, the ridges of any fingerprint left there turn white and come clearly into view. Another common method involves ninhydrin, which works like invisible ink: when you douse paper with it, the chemical brings out any sweat that may have been left by fingertips.

FBI fingerprint examiners have a variety of computer tools—a sort of specialized version of Photoshop—to help them compare prints with those in their system. But in the end only a human being can decide whether prints really match. This means a match is only as good as the knowledge, experience, and ability of the specialist who makes it.

There are also no standards for a match, even though fingerprint analysis has been in use for decades. How many distinct characteristics are necessary to prove a partial fingerprint comes from a specific person? The answer is different in New York, California, and London. **4**

So examining the many contours of a human finger is not as objective as scanning a bar code. But it's not guesswork, either. ○

4 Evaluating
What is your opinion of the usefulness of fingerprint evidence?

Answering the BIG Question

As you do the following activities, consider the Big Question:
What do you do when you don't know what to do?

WRITE TO LEARN Has reading this article changed your views on crime investigations? Answer this question in a brief entry in your Learner's Notebook.

PARTNER TALK With a partner, role-play a conversation that Shirley McKie might have had with a coworker who thought she was guilty of lying under oath.

The Five Little Foxes and the Tiger

retold by Kathleen Arnott

What do you do when you're faced with a hungry tiger?

Once upon a time, on the plains of East Pakistan, a fox and his wife lived in a snug little hole.

They had five children who were too young to feed themselves, and so every evening Mr. and Mrs. Fox crept out of their hole and made their way to the bazaar or market place, which was full of roughly-made stalls.

But they didn't go there to buy anything. They waited until all the people had gone home to their suppers, and then the two foxes crept amongst the stalls looking for scraps of food for their children.

Sometimes they found nothing but a few grains of rice or shreds of pumpkin but at other times they picked up quite large pieces of fish or meat which had been dropped unnoticed by a stall-holder.

Then the two foxes were overjoyed and would hurry home talking happily together.

But no matter who had found the most food—and to be truthful it was nearly always Mrs. Fox who was the better <u>scavenger</u>—Mr. Fox was so full of pride at his cleverness that he could not stop boasting.

"How much sense have you got, my dear?" he would ask his wife as they hurried along between large tufts of brown grass and withered-looking bushes.

"About as much as would fill a small vegetable basket," Mrs. Fox would reply modestly.

Then after a few minutes she would say, "And how much sense have you got, my good husband?"

"As much as would fill twelve large sacks, needing twelve strong oxen to carry them," the conceited Mr. Fox would reply, time and time again. **❶**

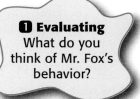

❶ Evaluating
What do you think of Mr. Fox's behavior?

Now one evening, when the two foxes were on their way home with food for their children, and Mr. Fox had just told his wife for the hundredth time how clever he was, a large tiger suddenly stepped out from behind a bush and barred their way.

"At last I've got you," growled the tiger, showing them his sharp white teeth which glistened in the moonlight.

Mr. Fox began to tremble and his legs gave way, so that he crumpled up into a heap and lost the power to speak.

But clever Mrs. Fox held her head high, and looking straight into the flashing eyes of the tiger, she said with a smile, "How glad we are to have met you, O Uncle! My husband and I have been having an

---

Vo•cab•u•lary

scavenger (SKAV in jur) person or animal that takes pieces of rubbish or decayed matter for its own use

argument, and since neither will give way to the other, we decided that we would ask the first superior animal who crossed our path to settle the matter for us."

The tiger was surprised at being spoken to so politely, and also very flattered at being called "Uncle," which is a term of great respect in Pakistan.

So he did not spring at the foxes to kill and eat them, but replied, "Very well. I will help you if I can. Tell me what you were arguing about."

"My husband and I have decided to part company," said Mrs. Fox in a clear, calm voice, while her husband, who had closed his eyes in fear, now opened them wide in surprise. "But we have five children waiting at home for us, and we cannot decide how to divide them between us fairly. I think that I should have three, since I have had to spend more time in looking after them than my husband, and that he should have only two. But my husband insists that I let him have the three boy-cubs, and that I keep only the two girl-cubs. Now, O wise Uncle, who do you think is right?"

When Mrs. Fox saw the tiger licking his lips she knew that he was thinking that somehow he must have the five fox cubs as well as their parents for his dinner. And this was exactly what she had hoped for.

"I must see the cubs for myself before I can make a decision," said the tiger. "Will you take me to your home?"

"Certainly," said Mrs. Fox. "We will lead the way, and you shall follow."

Poor Mr. Fox was completely at a loss to know what his wife was doing, but thinking that anything would be better than being eaten alive by a tiger, he staggered to his feet and followed his wife along the rough track, until they reached their home.

"Wait here," said Mrs. Fox to the tiger. "You are too big to get inside our hole, so we will bring the children outside for you to see."

She turned to her husband to tell him to go in, but he,

needing no encouragement to get away from the tiger, shot into the opening like a flash.

Mrs. Fox went in more slowly, talking all the time, saying that she would not keep him waiting more than a moment, and thanking him for being so gracious as to promise to judge their case for them.

Once inside their hole, the foxes gathered their children together as far away from the opening as possible, and in whispers told them what had happened.

"Don't make a sound," said Mrs. Fox, "and presently the tiger will realize he has been tricked, and will go away."

She was right. The tiger waited for hours, first patiently, then furiously, as it gradually dawned on him that the foxes had no intention of letting him see their children, and when the sun rose the next morning, he had to go hungrily away.

After this, Mr. and Mrs. Fox went by a different path to the bazaar, and kept a sharp look-out for tigers.

Mr. Fox never again asked his wife how much sense she had, but once or twice, when he showed signs of becoming proud again she would say to him, "How much sense have you got, my dear?" and he would answer with an embarrassed laugh, "Oh! About as much as would fill a small vegetable basket—a very small one, I'm afraid." ❷ ○

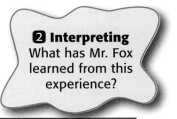

❷ **Interpreting**
What has Mr. Fox learned from this experience?

Answering the BIG Question

As you do the following activities, consider the Big Question:
What do you do when you don't know what to do?

WRITE TO LEARN Can you think of another way that Mrs. Fox might have outsmarted the tiger? In your Learner's Notebook, write an alternative ending to the story.

LITERATURE GROUPS Meet with two or three other students who have read this story. Discuss a time when you were in a scary situation. What did you do?

The Quality of Life—Your Choice to Be Free

by Sandra Lee Smith
from *Coping with Decision-Making*

Can young people work together to improve the looks of their neighborhood?

Every day you are confronted with many choices. There are daily activities to decide on, plans for your future to resolve, and the assortment of attitudes you elect to project. The way you cope with decision making shapes you into the unique individual that you are.

How you are perceived by the world is not a matter of circumstance, coincidence, or birth but how you *choose* to be perceived. The type of life you lead is what you have <u>decreed</u>. *You* are the only one who can determine your quality of life. The responsibility is yours.

Vo•cab•u•lary

decreed (dih KREED) made or announced a decision

Often it is difficult to believe you have much control over your life. But blaming circumstances or complaining continually will not resolve the situation. You must set your goals, decide on what action to take, and then assert yourself to do it. That is how you gain control. **❶**

Donna lived in a neighborhood where the families were poor. Her family barely scraped by on the disability checks her dad received from the Veterans Administration. Her mother managed to supplement the income by babysitting neighbors' children, but they couldn't pay much.

❶ Monitoring Comprehension According to the author, how can people gain control over their own lives?

Donna had many circumstances to blame her unhappiness on. Let's see what she decides to do.

Donna walked down the street and kicked the can someone had tossed out a car window. "I get so mad about all this litter. Why do people throw their garbage all around anyway? Just look at this, will you?"

Donna gestured at the packed dirt yards dotted with scraps of paper, bits of glass, and shiny aluminum.

"What do you expect?" her friend Judy commented. "Nobody in this neighborhood cares."

Donna halted and put her hands on her hips. "Why don't they care?" she asked.

Judy shrugged. "They're too poor, I guess. I mean, who has money to build fancy fences and buy stuff for the yard?"

"Who said anything about buying fancy stuff?" Donna asked. "All I want is clean yards and a nice-looking street. That doesn't cost anything. I mean, look at it." She gestured with a wide sweep of her hand. "Those big trees are great. This could be a really nice-looking place."

Donna continued walking down the tree-lined street, and Judy kept in step beside her.

Judy sighed. "When I grow up I'm going to move away from here and live in a house like Erin's. Isn't that the most?" **2**

Donna pictured the lovely home of their school friend. Erin lived on the far side of town where large homes stood amid stately gardens. For a few moments she allowed herself to dream wistfully, but then she shook off the fantasy and faced reality. Her street. It didn't have to be this way. Hadn't her history teacher taught them about taking political action? She could do that here.

2 Connecting
Do you spend much time envying what other people have?

Excitement began to churn inside Donna as she stopped again and pulled Judy beside her. "Remember what Mr. Lee said about making changes? Why don't we form a neighborhood action committee and get our own street looking nice?"

"What are you talking about? We can't do anything about this neighborhood."

"Sure we can. We can organize and form a plan. Then we'll go around to all the houses and ask everyone to help out." Donna started walking again, her steps brisk and purposeful. "We'll form a committee to clean up the trash. We can earn money to buy paint for the fences."

"Whoa there," Judy halted. "What if everyone doesn't want this? Can you just see ole man Harper letting us near his yard?"

"Don't be such a pessimist," Donna assured her. "Once he sees how nice the other yards will look, he'll come around."

"I may be a pessimist, but you're sure an optimist. There's no way you can pull this off."

Donna ignored Judy's lack of enthusiasm. She knew she could count on the Carter twins next door. The two boys had crushes on her and would do anything she asked. Their dad had a wheelbarrow too. He'd let them use it.

Then there were her two brothers. She'd make them help. If Judy would stop complaining long enough, Donna could probably talk her into getting her sister to join in.

Mentally, Donna listed all the people on the block that she could count on to cooperate. By the time she'd figured it out, she felt much more positive about her idea. Surely with that kind of manpower they could accomplish something. If nothing else, picking up the trash would help.

The next day at school, Donna approached Mr. Lee after class and told him of her plan. "Do you think it'll work?" she asked.

"Sure do," Mr. Lee smiled. "Sounds like an excellent idea, and it will benefit the community as well."

A sense of pride and happiness made Donna feel as if she could burst. "Do you have any ideas that might help?"

Mr. Lee settled back in his chair and drummed his fingers on his desk. "I think I could give you some pointers, and I have another idea. Why don't you make it your class project? You and your friends from your neighborhood that are in this class can work on it together, plan it, write it up as a report, and get credit for it as well."

Donna could barely believe it. Not only would she help solve the neighborhood problem, but she'd get her class report out of it. She hurried out of the classroom after saying good-bye to Mr. Lee. Wait until she told Judy and the others.

The project Donna has in mind will take a lot of effort, coordination, and planning to pull off successfully. Do you think she will be able to do so? It sounds overwhelming, but in fact the project is very <u>feasible</u> when carefully thought out.

Often we think we are victims of circumstances. Judy figured that because the neighborhood was poor it had to look trashed out. That is simply not true. There is no big rule book in the sky that says poor neighborhoods have to look a certain way. It is how the people in them *decide* they will look.

Vo•cab•u•lary

feasible (FEE zuh bul) possible

This concept applies to many circumstances you will find yourselves in during your lifetime. You can take several approaches. You can complain as Donna did. You can dream as Judy did and wish for change. Or you can observe the situation and take action. Which approach do you think will accomplish anything?

Complaining and daydreaming are options. If those are the courses of action you decide on, then the lack of change is the consequence *you* have to live with.

Action is an alternative that will produce more results if carefully planned and executed. Donna could have decided on a negative course of action, such as yelling at the neighbors, expressing her anger with graffiti, or trashing the place more in rebellion. But her decision was positive and constructive. What do you think the quality of Donna's life will be like? How about Judy? Which lifestyle would you prefer?

Electing to be an active or a passive citizen is one of the factors to consider in determining your quality of life. Another is knowing what is best for you and your being true to yourself. Often you can be pressured into decisions that you know are wrong for you. Assertive control of your own best interests is a necessary skill in coping with quality living. **3** ○

> **3 Evaluating**
> What is your opinion of the advice the author gives in this selection?

Answering the BIG Question

As you do the following activities, consider the Big Question:
What do you do when you don't know what to do?

WRITE TO LEARN Think about ways students could work together to improve the appearance of your school or school grounds. Write a brief entry in your Learner's Notebook about what you would like to accomplish.

LITERATURE GROUPS Meet with two or three other students who have read this selection. Discuss the Learner's Notebook entries you have written. Choose an idea that would be a good and feasible class project.

Angella D. Ferguson

by Robert C. Hayden
from *11 African American Doctors*

How can doctors help a patient who is too young to talk?

The tiny African-American baby girl had just been admitted to the hospital. Her hands and feet were painfully swollen. She lay in her hospital crib, first sobbing, then whimpering. Her swollen hands lay stiffly outstretched on the sheets. The child's mother hovered over the bed, helplessly watching her baby suffer while the doctors tried to find out what was wrong.

Angella D. Ferguson

The diagnosis was not slow in coming: sickle-cell anemia. The baby had inherited the incurable disease from her parents, just as she had inherited her brown skin. The mother's sorrow doubled. Not only was her baby very sick, but she and the baby's father had <u>unwittingly</u> given the baby the sickness.

Pain, suffering, and sorrowful, guilt-ridden parents—these are Dr. Angella Ferguson's first memories of sickle-cell anemia, the disease that she studied for nearly twenty years of her life. Ferguson was a young intern when she saw her first case of sickle-cell anemia.

As a medical student, she had learned that sickle-cell anemia is a disease that mainly afflicts black people. It was brought to the United States in the genes of enslaved Africans. The disease stems from a defect in the chemical structure of hemoglobin, the oxygen-carrying substance that gives blood its color. Such flawed hemoglobin is called hemoglobin-S.

When the body needs more oxygen than normal—when it is infected or fatigued, for instance—hemoglobin-S forms crystal-like rods in the blood cells. When this happens, normally donut-shaped red blood cells are <u>distorted</u> into sickle-like shaped cells. The misshapen blood cells clog the blood vessels. The disruption of the normal flow of life-giving blood results in pain, swelling, and damage to other organs in the body.

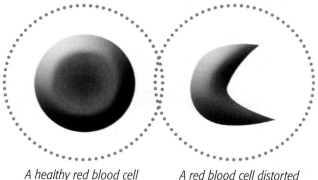

A healthy red blood cell　　　*A red blood cell distorted by sickle-cell anemia*

Vo•cab•u•lary

unwittingly (un WIT ing lee) without knowing or realizing
distorted (dih STOR tid) changed from normal condition

264　UNIT 4　What do you do when you don't know what to do?

People who have sickle-cell anemia have inherited the gene for hemoglobin-S from both parents. A person who inherits a hemoglobin-S gene from only one parent is said to have a sickle-cell trait. A person with a sickle-cell trait has a few of the red blood cells that carry hemoglobin-S, but he or she seldom has any problems. Such people may live most of their lives with no knowledge of the genetic trait they carry. ❶

Dr. Ferguson had learned this much about sickle-cell anemia in medical school. She was to add much more information to that body of knowledge.

Dr. Angella Ferguson chose a career in pediatrics, the branch of medicine that deals with the care of infants and children.

While studying healthy babies, Dr. Ferguson searched for ways to help those with sickle-cell anemia . . .

❶ **Monitoring Comprehension**
What is the difference between sickle-cell anemia and a sickle-cell trait?

Suffering Children

Dr. Ferguson had assigned herself a difficult task. She knew that sickle-cell anemia was inherited, so there could be no immediate hope of prevention. The only approach, it seemed, was to study the painful symptoms and find ways to relieve them.

For the sickle-cell victim, the most dangerous and painful time is called the crisis. Sickle-cell crises can strike at any time and in any part of the body. During such a crisis, the logjam of sickled cells cuts off the flow of blood through blood vessels, triggering such symptoms as pain and swelling due to the blocking up of body fluids. Other symptoms, such as skin ulcers and brain damage, may be the result of tissue dying for lack of nourishing blood. Thus, sickle-cell crises can mimic other sicknesses such as heart attack, pneumonia, and even strokes.

Sorting Out the Symptoms

Sorting through the symptoms, Dr. Ferguson and her research team managed to classify the symptoms by age groups. They found that from birth to two years, most sickle-cell victims suffered arthritic-like symptoms of pain and swelling in the joints, especially the ankles and wrists.

From age two to six, abdominal pains were the most frequent symptoms. These pains were due to the swelling of internal organs, such as the liver and the spleen, which also caused the child to develop a potbelly.

From age six to twelve, the symptoms grew milder. But at age twelve, as the child's body began to mature, the disease often flared up again. It was then that the sickle-cell victim often developed ulcers on the legs.

These symptoms, however, did not always provide a reliable guide for detecting a victim. One tragic case that Dr. Ferguson treated was that of a six-year-old boy who seemed perfectly well until he had his tonsils removed. The anesthesia used during the operation brought on a sickle-cell crisis that affected his brain. The boy was unconscious and paralyzed for several days. Then, slowly, he regained consciousness and the use of his body. But over the next eighteen months, he had four more brain crises. Finally, he died. The <u>autopsy</u> showed a brain that was almost completely destroyed by the disease. Yet the boy had not shown the slightest sign of having sickle-cell anemia until his tonsils were removed.

Even out of this tragedy, medical researchers learned something new about sickle-cell anemia. They learned that the sickle-cell victim must be given a great deal of oxygen after surgery in order to prevent a crisis.

Avoiding the Crisis

Now having tracked down the symptoms of sickle-cell anemia, Dr. Ferguson turned her attention to the cause of the crisis itself. A diary kept on each patient provided a day-by-day account of the health happenings in each child's life. Then, when a sickle-cell crisis developed, Dr. Ferguson simply consulted the diary for clues as to what might have brought on the attack. Quite often the cause was an infection.

Vo·cab·u·lary

autopsy (AW top see) surgery to find the cause of death

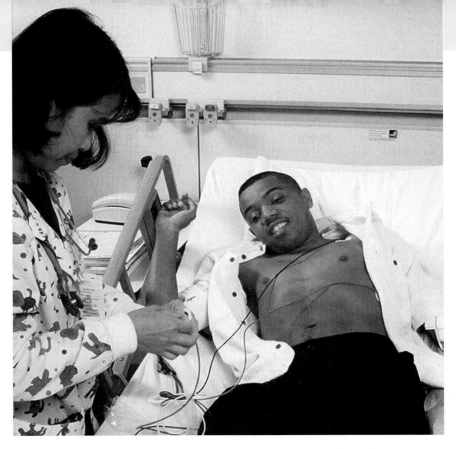

A young sickle-cell anemia patient receives a blood transfusion.

Laboratory tests on the children revealed two other important clues. The blood of the sickle-cell victim in crisis was thicker and often more <u>acidic</u> than it should have been. Using this information as a guide, Dr. Ferguson set about finding ways to prevent sickle-cell crisis.

She began by attacking the problem of thick blood. Giving fluids through a needle in the vein thinned out the blood. But Ferguson found that simply having the child drink large amounts of water achieved the same effect. She enlisted the parents in the water project. They were advised to keep a jug of water in the

---

Vo•cab•u•lary

acidic (uh SID ik) containing a great deal of acid

refrigerator for the child. Dr. Ferguson would say to the mother, "Tell your child, 'Drink that jug empty.'"

Since drinking so much water could produce another problem, teachers were requested to let the child go to the bathroom as often as necessary. Dr. Ferguson also learned that adding small amounts of bicarbonate, an alkaline substance, to the drinking water seemed to adjust the acidity of the blood. ❷

> **❷ Interpreting**
> How would you describe Dr. Ferguson's approach to her work?

Sickle-cell patients were put on a program of infection prevention. Children were kept away from people suffering from even minor infections. Colds were attacked head-on with nose drops and other medicines. A balanced diet and vitamins built up the children's resistance to infection. Personal hygiene problems, such as dental work, were taken care of when the child was feeling well.

"The Whole Child"

Out of this beginning grew a guide for treating the child. "We treat the whole child: the student, the family member, as well as the child in crisis," said Dr. Ferguson. ○

Answering the BIG Question

As you do the following activities, consider the Big Question:
What do you do when you don't know what to do?

WRITE TO LEARN Think about the fact that Dr. Ferguson tackled one problem at a time with sickle-cell anemia. Then write a brief entry in your Learner's Notebook about how this approach allowed Ferguson to make real progress in the treatment of sickle-cell anemia.

LITERATURE GROUPS Meet with two or three other students who have read this selection. Discuss why you think Dr. Ferguson is so dedicated to treating patients with sickle-cell anemia.

BRAZILIAN PROGRAM SENDS KIDS TO SCHOOL

NOT WORK

by Karen Fanning

Some kids find an alternative to spending their days in a trash dump.

W hen Tatiana Alves de Oliveira was just a few months old, her desperately poor mother had no choice but to bring her baby daughter to work with her at the Alvarenga dump. As Tatiana lay under a piece of cardboard to shelter her from the sun, her mother rummaged through toxic heaps of trash in search of items she could resell. On good days, she also managed to find scraps of food—spoiled leftovers that would quiet her hunger pains. Now ten, Tatiana reflects back on her earlier days in the dump.

"There was lots of smoke, and it was dangerous," says the young girl from Sao Bernardo do Campo, a city outside of Sao Paolo, Brazil. "It could kill you. There were snakes and rats." **❶**

Fortunately, Tatiana is no longer forced to dodge filthy rodents or inhale toxic fumes. She's one of the lucky ones—one of nearly 47,000 children who have left the dumps within the past four years and now attend school. Yet, an estimated 40,000 children still remain trapped in the hazardous wastelands.

> **❶ Monitoring Comprehension**
> Describe the conditions at the Alvarenga dump.

"Children run the risk of being run down by the trucks and by the <u>compacting machine</u>," says Téia Magalhães, executive secretary of the National Forum Lixo e Cidadania. "They also have some skin problems and respiratory problems because they inhale the gases. It's a very high risk in terms of their health."

In July 2001, the government of Brazil closed the Alvarenga dump and replaced it with recycling centers. Today, Tatiana's mother works at the Ecology Recycling Center in Sao Bernardo do Campo, recycling metal, plastic, paper, and glass. For her labor,

Vo·cab·u·lary

compacting machine (com PAK ting muh SHEEN) device that packs pieces of trash together tightly to save space

she pockets nearly $100 a month, three times what she used to earn at the dump.

Instead of tagging along with her mother to work, Tatiana now attends school, thanks to a government-sponsored program called Bolsa Escola, which provides a small sum of money—a scholarship, of sorts—to parents so that their children can go to school.

Tatiana spends her mornings studying math, history, science, and Portuguese. In the afternoon she attends a local community center, where she takes computer classes, plays soccer, and learns to draw and dance.

Tatiana's mother is grateful for the opportunity her children have to get an education—an opportunity she never had.

"I'm so happy because they are able to learn things," says the 24-year-old. "I didn't have time to study. I only had time to work. I want them to have a better profession than mine. I want them to have a better future."

Tatiana wants a better future, too. After college, she hopes to become a school principal. In the meantime, she feels fortunate that she has the chance to learn.

"I like to read and write," she says. "I like to do my homework. It's a miracle that I'm learning how to do things." **2** ○

> **2 Interpreting**
> What is Tatiana's attitude toward education?

Answering the BIG Question

As you do the following activities, consider the Big Question:
What do you do when you don't know what to do?

WRITE TO LEARN Think about the job Tatiana's mother used to have. Why are human beings sometimes forced to work under such horrible conditions? Write your thoughts about this issue in your Learner's Notebook.

PARTNER TALK Get together with another student who has read the article. Talk about Tatiana's ambitions now that she is in school. Discuss how getting an education can make a difference in a young person's life.

STAYING Calm

by Elise O'Shaughnessy

When the first plane hit, Victoria Cross Kelly was in the middle of a breakfast meeting on the <u>concourse</u> level, below ground, at the World Trade Center. Kelly, deputy director of the PATH rail system that links New Jersey and New York City, had no idea what had happened. But she and her <u>colleagues</u> knew something was seriously wrong when they saw people stampeding out of the building. She hurried up an escalator to a street exit and saw a blizzard of paper— "My first thought was of a ticker-tape parade"—and more people running. "I figured I really needed to get back downstairs and get in touch with the PATH train master," Kelly says.

Police officers were pushing people out of the building, yelling, "Go! Go! Get out now!," but she turned right around and headed for the phone that would give her a direct line to the man running the trains. She quickly described what she was seeing, and they decided to halt or reroute all service to the trade center. ❶

Everyone—from her colleagues to the governor of New Jersey—credits Kelly, 49, with helping to save thousands of rush-hour commuters from the death trap the World Trade Center would become. Though this was her second brush with disaster there—she was working at the trade center when it was bombed in 1993 and six of her coworkers were killed—Kelly remained astonishingly cool.

She knew she couldn't leave yet. Her call had stopped the incoming trains, but two more were just entering the station. And so, while <u>chaos</u> reigned and a second plane slammed into the south tower, Kelly anxiously waited below street level until she

> ❶ **Monitoring Comprehension**
> Why did Kelly reenter the building?

Vo•cab•u•lary

concourse (KON kors) a large, open space for crowds to pass through
colleagues (KOL leegz) coworkers
chaos (KAY us) confusion

Police officers directed people to safety when the World Trade Center was attacked.

was certain that every PATH passenger—some 1,500 to 2,000 people—had been safely evacuated from the station. "I wasn't thinking about much at that point except wanting to be sure that there were no more people coming off the trains," she says now. "I really wasn't thinking about me or what was happening." Only when Kelly left at around 9:15 a.m. and started walking north, wondering how she was going to get back to her New Jersey office, did she see that both towers were on fire. A few blocks later, she stopped to get a glass of water at a restaurant. From a television there, she finally learned the full horror of the morning. And finally, she says, she felt fear.

Her husband had to tell their seven-year-old daughter what had happened; with all the emergency planning that needed to be done, Kelly didn't get home from PATH headquarters until 2:00 a.m. the next day. "My daughter was mostly upset about my working nights for a week," she says. "She didn't see me much. I would stop by her school on my way home from work just to see her awake!"

The World Trade Center PATH station was buried under tons of rubble. Weeks later, police surveying the scene found an empty train that had been badly damaged, several of its cars flattened by the collapse of the south tower. Mercifully, no one was inside. ○

Answering the BIG Question

As you do the following activities, consider the Big Question:
What do you do when you don't know what to do?

WRITE TO LEARN Think about the situation Victoria Cross Kelly suddenly faced when the first plane hit the World Trade Center. In your Learner's Notebook write a brief entry telling what you think you might have done in that same situation.

LITERATURE GROUPS Meet with two or three other students who have read this selection. Discuss what might have happened had Victoria not disobeyed the police officer's order to evacuate the building.

Index of Authors and Titles

Index of Authors and Titles

Acknowledgments

Literature credits

Unit 1

"I Absolutely Did Not Fit In" from *Got Issues Much: Celebrities Share Their Traumas and Triumphs*, by Randi Reisfeld and Marie Morreale. Copyright © 1995 by Randi Reisfeld and Marie Morreale. Reprinted by permission of Scholastic, Inc.

Reprinted with the permission of Scribner, an imprint of Simon & Schuster Adult Publishing Group, from *Cross Creek* by Marjorie Kinnan Rawlings. Copyright © 1942 by Marjorie Kinnan Rawlings; copyright renewed © 1970 by Norton Baskin and Charles Scribner's Sons.

"42nd Street Library" from *Jazmin's Notebook* by Nikki Grimes, copyright © 1998 by Nikki Grimes. Used by permission of Dial Books for Young Readers, A Division of Penguin Young Readers Group, A Member of Penguin Group (USA) inc., 345 Hudson Street, New York, NY 10014. All rights reserved.

"Companion" by Manjush Dasgupta. Reprinted by permission of Mrs. Sarbari Dasgupta.

"The List" from *A Maze Me: Poems for Girls* by Naomi Shihab Nye. Copyright © 2005 by Naomi Shihab Nye. Reprinted by permission of the author.

"My Robot" by Steven Maxwell.

"Bodies of Pompeii" by Jason Urbanus, from DIG's March 2005 issue: *Pompeii*, copyright © 2005, Carus Publishing Company, published by Cobblestone Publishing, 30 Grove Street, Suite C, Peterborough, NH 03458. All rights reserved. Used by permission of the publisher.

From *Maizon at Blue Hill* by Jacqueline Woodson. Copyright © 1992 by Jacqueline Woodson. Reprinted by permission of the Charlotte Sheedy Literary Agency.

"Jumping Over Boundaries" by Linda Alvarado. Copyright © 2005 by Highlights for Children, Inc., Columbus, Ohio. Reprinted by permission.

From *The Phantom Tollbooth* by Norton Juster, illustrated by Jules Feiffer, copyright © 1961 and renewed 1989 by Norton Juster; Illustrations copyright © 1961 and renewed 1989 by Jules Feiffer. Used by permission of Random House Children's Books, a division of Random House, Inc.

"Games to Take Your Breath Away" from BBC News.

Excerpt from *The Dawn of Aviation* by Tamra Orr. Copyright © 2005 by Mitchell Lane Publishers, Inc. Reprinted by permission.

"My Poems" by Alan Barlow, from *Rising Voices: Writings of Young Native Americans*.

"The Pen" by Muhammad al-Ghuzzi, translated by May Jayyusi and John Heath-Stubbs, from *Modern Arabic Poetry: An Anthology*, edited by Salma Khadra Jayyusi, copyright © 1987 by Columbia University Press. Reprinted with the permission of the publisher.

"Reply to the Question: 'How Can You Become a Poet?'" from *Rainbow Writing* by Eve Merriam. Copyright © 1976 by Eve Merriam. All Rights Reserved. Used by permission of Marian Reiner.

Unit 2

"The Game" from *Fast Sam, Cool Clyde and Stuff* by Walter Dean Myers. Reprinted by permission of Miriam Altshuler Literary Agency, on behalf of Walter Dean Myers. Copyright © 1975 by Walter Dean Myers.

"Tornado" from *National Geographic Kids*, June 2003. Reprinted by permission of the National Geographic Society.

"Drumbeats and Bullets" from *The Boys' War* by Jim Murphy. Text copyright © 1990 by Jim Murphy. Reprinted by permission of Clarion Books, an imprint of Houghton Mifflin Company. All rights reserved.

"Tomás Rivera" by Pat Mora is reprinted with permission from the publisher of *Riding Low on the Streets of Gold* by Judith Ortiz Cofer (Houston: Arte Publico Press—University of Houston © 2003).

Acknowledgments

"By Accident" by Jane O. Wayne. Reprinted by permission of the author.

"A Dog with Heart" by Sally Deneen. From *Dog Fancy*, July 2005. Reprinted with permission of the author.

"The Little Old House in Allermo" by Bizet Kizcorn.

"Soap Box Derby Puts Kids' Creativity, Racing Skills to the Test" Copyright © 2005 *Weekly Reader* Corporation. Reprinted by permission.

"The End of the World" by Jenny Leading Cloud, from *Glencoe Reader's Choice, Course 1*.

"Smoke Signals" by Eva Chen. Copyright © 2005 Conde Nast Publications. All rights reserved. Originally published in *Teen Vogue*. Reprinted by permission.

"Number One" words and music by Joni Mitchell. Copyright © 1988 Crazy Crow Music. All rights reserved. Used by permission.

From *Treasure Island* by Aurand Harris, from the book by Robert Louis Stevenson. Copyright © 1983 by Anchorage Press. Reprinted by permission of Anchorage Press Plays, Inc. www.applays.com

Unit 3

"Branded Beauty" from *In Your Face* by Shari Graydon. Copyright © 2004 by Shari Graydon. Reprinted by permission of Annick Press.

"Chuy's Beginnings" from *Finding Our Way* by René Saldaña, Jr., copyright © 2003 by René Saldaña, Jr. Used by permission of Random House Children's Books, a division of Random House, Inc.

"'I Escaped the Taliban'" by Kristin Baird Rattini. *National Geographic Kids* June/July 2005. Copyright © 2005 National Geographic Society. Reprinted by permission.

"The Ravine" by Graham Salisbury. Copyright © 2000 by Graham Salisbury.

"Military Tests May Harm Whales, Study Says" by Sarah Ives. *National Geographic Kids News*, November 4, 2003. Copyright © 2003 National Geographic Society. Reprinted by permission.

"Ragnar's Rock" by Douglas Holgate.

Excerpts "Little Man" and "History Repeating (Almost)" from *The Way a Door Closes* by Hope Anita Smith. Copyright © 2003 by Hope Anita Smith. Reprinted by permission of Henry Holt and Company, LLC.

"To Malcolm X" by Julius Thompson, from *Hopes Tied Up in Promises*. Copyright © 1970 by Julius Thompson.

"The Raiders Jacket" from *Local News*, copyright © 1993 by Gary Soto, reprinted by permission of Harcourt, Inc.

"The Monkey's Paw" adaptation by Harriet Dexter, from *Plays, The Drama Magazine for Young People*, reprinted with the permission of the publisher, Plays/Sterling Partners, Inc. Copyright © 1983 *Plays*, PO Box 600160, Newton, MA 02460.

Unit 4

"Honor Thy Father" by Dale Earnhardt Jr., from *Dale Earnhardt Jr.: Driven by Destiny*, by Mark Stewart. Copyright © 2003 by Bittersweet Publishing, Inc. Published by The Millbrook Press, Inc.

Reprinted with the permission of Atheneum Books for Young Readers, an imprint of Simon & Schuster Children's Publishing Division from *Hatchet* by Gary Paulsen. Copyright © 1987 by Gary Paulsen.

Excerpt from *Crime Lab 101* by Robert Gardner. Copyright © 1992 by Robert Gardner. Reprinted by permission of Bloomsbury Publishing.

From "Dolphin Rescue" by Gail Hennessey. Published in *Scholastic News Online*, September 24, 2005. *Teacher.Scholastic*. Copyright © 2005, 2006 by Scholastic Inc. Reprinted by permission.

"The Calamity Kids in The Time Loop Locket!" by Sara Turner and Jerzy Drozd.

"History Repeating (Almost)" by Hope Anita Smith, from *The Way A Door Closes*. Copyright © 1993 by Hope Anita Smith. Published by Henry Holt and Co.

Excerpt from *Cry of Courage* by Lee Roddy. Published by Mott Media. Copyright © 1998 by Lee Roddy. Reprinted by permission.

"There Isn't Time" by Eleanor Farjeon. Reprinted with permission of Harold Ober Associates Incorporated, from *Poems for Children*. Copyright © 1933, 1961 by Eleanor Farjoen.

"Do Fingerprints Lie?" by Michael Specter. Reprinted by permission of International Creative Management. Copyright © 2005 by Michael Specter.

"The Five Little Foxes and the Tiger" retold by Kathleen Arnott, from *Animal Folk Tales Around the World.* Copyright © 1970 by Kathleen Arnott. Published by Henry Z. Walck.

Excerpt from *Coping With Decision-Making* by Sandra Lee Smith. Copyright © 1989 by Sandra Lee Smith. Reprinted by permission of The Rosen Publishing Group.

"Angella D. Ferguson" by Robert C. Hayden, from *11 African American Doctors.* Copyright © 1992 by Robert C. Hayden. Published by Twenty-First Century Books.

From "Child Labor Around the World: Brazilian Program Sends Kids to School, Not Work" by Karen Fanning. Published in *Scholastic News In-Depth Online,* September 24, 2005. *Teacher.Scholastic.* Copyright © 2005, 2006 by Scholastic, Inc. Reprinted by permission.

"Staying Calm" *from* "Finding the hero in you" by Elise O'Shaughnessy, from *Good Housekeeping,* January 2002. Copyright © 2002 Hearst Communications, Inc.

Glencoe would like to acknowledge the artists who participated in illustrating this program: Steven Maxwell; Bizet Kizcorn; Douglas Holgate; Sara Turner and Jerzy Drozd.

Photo credits

Cover i (t)2006 JupiterImages Corporation/photos.com, (c)Artville, (bl)Getty Images, (br)Jason Reed/Getty Images; **iv v** Cut and Deal Ltd./Index Open; **0** (inset)2006 JupiterImages Corporation/photos.com, (inset)Getty Images, (bkgd)2006 JupiterImages Corporation/photos.com, (bkgd)AbleStock/Index Open, (bkgd)DesignPics/Index Open, (bkgd)DesignPics/Index Open, (bkgd)photos.com/Index Open; **2** Neal Preston/CORBIS; **5** Jose Luis Pelaez, Inc./Getty Images; **6** Image100 Ltd.; **8** FogStock/Index Open; **13** (bkgd)Ryan McVay/Getty Images, (inset)2006 JupiterImages Corporation/photos.com; **14** FogStock/Index Open; **16** (t)Neil Beer/Getty Images, (c)Stockbyte/Punchstock Images, (b)2006 JupiterImages Corporation/photos.com; **17** 2006 JupiterImages Corporation/photos.com; **18** (inset) 2006 JupiterImages Corporation/photos.com, (bkgd)Digital Vision;

19 Getty Images; **33** Roger Ressmeyer/CORBIS; **34** Mark Polott/IndexOpen; **36** 2006 JupiterImages Corporation/photos.com; **40** Comstock/PunchStock; **43** Carolyn A. Herter/Knight-Ridder/Tribune Media Information Services; **44** FogStock/Index Open; **46** Getty Images; **51** Jason Reed/Getty Images; **52** Comstock/PunchStock; **56** Keith Brofsky/Getty Images; **57** Library of Congress; **58** 2006 JupiterImages Corporation/photos.com; **60** Doug Menuez/Getty Images; **61** Getty Images; **63** 2006 JupiterImages Corporation/photos.com; **64** Andy Sotiriou/Getty Images; **65** Getty Images; **66** (inset)CORBIS, (bkgd)C Squared Studios/Getty Images; **69** (bkgd)C Squared Studios/Getty Images, (inset)CORBIS; **70** Jim Mone/AP/Wide World Photos, THE REPORTER, Don Lloyd/AP/Wide World Photos; **71** C Squared Studios/Getty Images; **75** CORBIS; **77** AP/Wide World Photos; **79** (bkgd)Stockbyte/PictureQuest, (inset)Used by permission of Special Collections, University of California, Riverside Libraries, University of California, Riverside, CA; **80** Stockbyte/PictureQuest; **81** Colin Anderson/Brand X Pictures/jupiterimages; **82** CORBIS; **83** G.K. & Vicki Hart/Getty Images; **84** Getty Images; **86** Comstock/Alamy; **99 100** Tom E. Puskar/AP/Wide World Photos; **101** (inset)CORBIS, (bkgd)Brand X Pictures/Punchstock; **102 103** CORBIS; **104** Creatas/Punchstock; **105** C. Sherburne/Getty Images; **105 106** Creatas/Punchstock; **107** Keith Brofsky/Getty Images; **108** (t)Creatas/Punchstock, (b)Janis Christie/Getty Images; **109** (inset)Steve Cole/Getty Images, (bkgd)Digital Vision/Punchstock; **111** Adam Nadel/AP/Wide World Photos; **112** Mary Evans Picture Library/Alamy; **113** Joshua Ets-Hokin/Getty Images; **114 115 116 117** Getty Images; **118** (inset)Comstock/Alamy, (bkgd)Getty Images; **120** (bkgd)Getty Images, (inset)Janis Christie/Getty Images; **121** Getty Images; **122** (inset)CORBIS, (bkgd)Getty Images; **124 125** Getty Images; **125** Spike Mafford/Getty Images; **126** (inset) Julie Delton/Getty Images, (bkgd)Getty Images; **127** (inset)C Squared Studios/Getty Images, (bkgd)Getty Images; **130 131** Getty Images; **132** photos.com; **134** Artville; **136** BananaStock/Punchstock; **137** ImageSource/PictureQuest; **139** Getty Images; **141** SW Productions/Getty Images; **142** Artville; **144** Tomas Munita/AP/World Wide Photos; **146** Wallace Garrison/Index Open; **149** Glen Allison/Getty Images; **151** CORBIS; **153** FogStock/Index Open; **155** S. Solum/Getty Images; **157** DesignPics/Index Open; **159** Getty Images; **173** RubberBall;

Acknowledgments

175 Time Life Pictures/Getty Images; **176 178 180** Getty Images; **183** (l)Stockbyte, (r)Ryan McVay/Getty Images; **184 186** Getty Images; **188** Digital Vision; **190** (inset)Hot Ideas/Index Open, (bkgd)Digital Vision; **193** Getty Images; **195 196** CORBIS; **199** Getty Images; **200** (inset)Don Farrall/Getty Images, (bkgd)Index Open; **203** Image Source, photo library. com/IndexOpen; **204 206** Getty Images; **207** IndexOpen; **208** Brand X Pictures/ Punchstock; **210** Donovan Reese/Getty Images; **213** 2006 JupiterImages Corporation/ photos.com; **215** Nicki Nikoni/Getty Images; **217** Chad Baker/Getty Images; **218** (inset)C. Sherburne/Getty Images, (bkgd)2006 JupiterImages Corporation /photos.com; **220** 2006 JupiterImages Corporation /photos. com; **235** Steve Cole/Getty Images; **237** (inset)2006 JupiterImages Corporation/photos. com, (bkgd)Barry Winkler/Getty Images; **239** Charlie Borland; **240 241** Getty Images; **243** Brownie Harris/CORBIS; **245** AbleStock/Index Open; **246 251 252** Getty Images; **254** (inset)CORBIS, (bkgd)Siede Preis/Getty Images; **256** Getty Images; **258** (inset)Keith Levit Photography, (bkgd)S. Meltzer/Getty Images; **260** (inset) BananaStock/PunchStock, (bkgd)SW Productions/Getty Images; **263** CORBIS; **267** Grantpix/IndexOpen; **269** (l)Tracy Montana/Getty Images, (r)Digital Vision; **270** Comstock/Alamy; **272** AFP/Getty Images; **274** REUTERS/Dylan Martinez/CORBIS; **275** Paul Colangelo/CORBIS.